New Daylight

Edited by Naomi Starkey   January–April 2007

Suggestions for using *New Daylight*

Find a regular time and place, if possible, where you can read and pray undisturbed. Before you begin, take time to be still and perhaps use the BRF prayer. Then read the Bible passage slowly (try reading it aloud if you find it over-familiar), followed by the comment. You can also use *New Daylight* for group study and discussion, if you prefer.

The prayer or point for reflection can be a starting point for your own meditation and prayer. Many people like to keep a journal to record their thoughts about a Bible passage and items for prayer. In *New Daylight* we also note the Sundays and special festivals from the Church calendar, to keep in step with the Christian year.

New Daylight and the Bible

New Daylight contributors use a range of Bible versions, and you will find a list of the versions used in each issue at the back of the notes on page 154. You are welcome to use your own preferred version alongside the passage printed in the notes, and this can be particularly helpful if the Bible text has been abridged.

New Daylight affirms that the whole of the Bible is God's revelation to us, and we should read, reflect on and learn from every part of both Old and New Testaments. Usually the printed comment presents a straight-forward 'thought for the day', but sometimes it may also raise questions rather than simply providing answers, as we wrestle with some of the more difficult passages of Scripture.

Writers in this issue

David Winter is retired from parish ministry. An honorary Canon of Christ Church, Oxford, he is well known as a writer and broadcaster. He is a Series Editor of *The People's Bible Commentary*.

Jennifer Oldroyd worked for many years at the Ashburnham Place conference centre in East Sussex. She was Managing Editor for a major Christian publisher, and in the last few years has had two books published of study material for small groups.

Veronica Zundel is an Oxford graduate, writer and journalist. She lives with her husband and young son in North London, where they belong to the Mennonite Church.

Helen Julian CSF is an Anglican Franciscan sister, a member of the Community of St Francis, and presently serving as Minister Provincial for her community. She has written *Living the Gospel* and *The Road to Emmaus* for BRF.

Stephen Rand has given much of his time over recent years to his role as co-chair of Jubilee Debt Campaign, while he and his wife Susan have also been part of the leadership team of a young and small Baptist church in Wimbledon that meets to worship in the local Odeon cinema! Stephen was the author of BRF's 2006 Advent book *When the Time was Right*.

Gordon Giles is a vicar in Enfield, north-west London, previously based at St Paul's Cathedral, where his work involved musical and liturgical responsibilities. Trained in music, philosophy and theology, he was ordained in the Anglican Church in 1995.

Tony Horsfall is a freelance trainer and associate of EQUIP, a missions programme based at Bawtry Hall near Doncaster. He is an elder of his local church in West Yorkshire, and regularly travels abroad leading retreats and Quiet Days. He has written *Song of the Shepherd* and *A Fruitful Life* for BRF.

Jane Cornish is the 2000 winner of the Shelagh Brown Memorial Prize. She has been writing group study notes for many years for her local Anglican church and is now training for local lay ministry.

Anne Roberts trained in Wales as a geographer and teacher and taught in Uganda for two years. Having worked for a large Anglican church for many years, she is now a freelance writer and works in church administration and Further Education teaching and administration.

Further BRF reading for this issue

For more in-depth coverage of some of the passages in these Bible reading notes, we recommend the following titles:

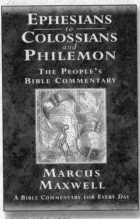

1 84101 047 2, £7.99

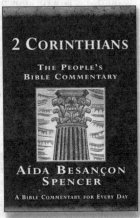

1 84101 073 1, £7.99

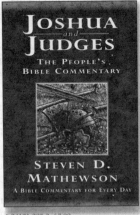

1 84101 095 2, £7.99

1 84101 065 0, £7.99

Naomi Starkey writes...

I'd like to begin this first 2007 issue of *New Daylight* by welcoming a new contributor to the team: Jennifer Oldroyd, whose opening set of readings is an in-depth study of Isaiah 40. This is possibly one of the best-loved passages in the Old Testament, with a great depth of compassion and consolation, and it is good to be able to dwell on it, verse by verse, over seven days.

On one day, Jennifer invites us to reflect on a related New Testament passage—not printed out because of space restraints—and this gives me an opportunity for an important reminder. While 'Bible passage included' is a long-standing feature of these notes, this does not mean that we should never open our Bibles alongside our copies of *New Daylight*! While I aim to include as much of the designated passage as possible, many bits of the Bible need abridging in order to provide a coherent chunk for comment. I appreciate that it is probably a bit too challenging to juggle *New Daylight*, open Bible (and possibly umbrella, newspaper, briefcase, etc) on a crowded train (or wherever/whenever you read the notes). It would be a shame, though, only ever to read the 'digested' version and not give ourselves the chance to check out the full text.

Also in this issue, we have David Winter with an overview of Philippians, a letter overflowing with love and gratitude. As David concludes in his introduction, 'If I was recommending a letter of Paul's to a first-time reader of the New Testament, it would be this one!'

Tony Horsfall brings to an end our readings in Judges, without doubt one of the darkest corners of the Bible. It is fitting, then, that immediately after the grim conclusion of that book ('In those days Israel had no king; everyone did as he saw fit'), we come to Jane Cornish's readings for Holy Week and Easter. With passages this year from John's Gospel, we follow the story of Jesus' suffering, death and resurrection, with its amazing promise of forgiveness extending even to those who perpetrate atrocities such as the events recounted in the book of Judges.

And in the days after Easter, we can come before God and express the highs and lows of our lives in the words of the Psalms. Anne Roberts spends two weeks looking at passages from Psalms 107—150, a mixture of light and shade, grieving and rejoicing.

The BRF Prayer

Almighty God,
you have taught us that your word is a lamp for our feet
and a light for our path. Help us, and all who prayerfully
read your word, to deepen our fellowship with each other
through your love. And in so doing may we come to know you
more fully, love you more truly, and follow more faithfully in
the steps of your son Jesus Christ, who lives and reigns with
you and the Holy Spirit, one God for evermore. Amen.

Philippians

The letters of Paul are part of the Christian scriptures, bound up with the Gospels, Acts, Revelation and various other letters in the collection of books we call 'the New Testament'. That's fine, but the danger is we may forget that these are *letters*, from one man to another group of people. Like all letters, they deal with the matters in hand, sometimes arising from questions or needs that the church has already communicated to him.

The style is very much that of other correspondence from this era—a bit more formal than most of our letters today, and addressed to more than one person, with the clear intention that they should be read aloud. Philippians was written (probably in about AD55) to the church at Philippi, a town in northeast Greece founded by Mark Anthony in 41BC as a colony for veterans of his victorious army. It was governed as a municipality of a Roman province, but the population would have been racially mixed, including some Jews—but not enough male Jews to form a synagogue. Hence some (Jewish) 'believers' gathered on the Sabbath by the river at a 'place of prayer', where Paul and Silas preached to them and saw Lydia, a Gentile attracted to Judaism, become the first Christian convert in Europe.

Philippians was written from prison (see 1:13). Earlier commentators assumed it was from Rome, towards the end of Paul's life, but most now reckon it was at Ephesus during the mid-50s AD. It is probably the most affectionate of Paul's letters, with a note of intimacy and warmth throughout, even when he has to rebuke two women workers for breaking unity. There's a good chance that we know the identity of the addressee of this letter, Syzygus (4:3)—though the NRSV rather pedantically translates this as 'companion', which is what the word means. He thanks the Philippians for their generosity, faithfulness and commitment to the gospel of Christ.

Those who only think of Paul as a rather thin-lipped kill-joy and misogynist can't have read this letter, full of love and gratitude for the people who made up this outpost of the gospel. This was a church whose first member was a woman and in which, judging by the greetings towards the end, women had always played a major role in its life and ministry. If I was recommending a letter of Paul's to a first-time reader of the New Testament, it would be this one!

David Winter

Praying with joy

Paul and Timothy, servants of Christ Jesus, To all the saints in Christ Jesus who are in Philippi, with the bishops and deacons: Grace to you and peace from God our Father and the Lord Jesus Christ. I thank my God every time I remember you, constantly praying with joy in every one of my prayers for all of you, because of your sharing in the gospel from the first day until now. I am confident of this, that the one who began a good work among you will bring it to completion by the day of Jesus Christ.

The church at Philippi came into being with a visit by Paul, the conversion of a wealthy business-woman and a terrified jailer in an earthquake. No wonder he remembered them 'constantly' (v. 4)! As a church, they were obviously active in evangelism ('sharing in the gospel', v. 5). That 'sharing' was not simply a matter of witnessing to the unbelievers, but expresses their 'fellowship' or 'communion' (all valid translations of the same word) with Paul and each other.

That community, he says, is 'the saints in Christ Jesus who are at Philippi' (v. 1). There's a whole world of truth in that one sentence! They were 'saints', not in the stained-glass window sense, but as those who through their faith in Jesus were being made holy. But they weren't to see that as an otherworldly thing. They were 'in Christ', but also 'in Philippi'. It was there, in that place, that they were to reflect the life of Christ. Equally, you and I are the 'saints in Christ', wherever we are.

In view of all this, it's not surprising that Paul prays for them 'with joy' (v. 4). His prayer for them is 'constant', which suggests it was at least regular and possibly daily, and it is motivated by his memory of their fellowship 'from the first day' (v. 5) until now. In other words, from the time of Lydia's conversion until the present day they had continued in this work. There had been no slackening of effort, no loss of enthusiasm. The Philippians would be good models for any church today!

Reflection

Paul's confidence is that what God begins, he completes—a wonderfully reassuring thought when we are tempted to think that our Christian life is sinking without trace!

DW

Overflowing love

It is right for me to think this way about all of you, because you hold me in your heart, for all of you share in God's grace with me, both in my imprisonment and in the defence and confirmation of the gospel. For God is my witness, how I long for all of you with the compassion of Christ Jesus. And this is my prayer, that your love may overflow more and more with knowledge and full insight to help you to determine what is best, so that in the day of Christ you may be pure and blameless, having produced the harvest of righteousness that comes through Jesus Christ for the glory and praise of God.

Perhaps this is how we should all pray for our fellow Christians! Paul emphasizes what they have in common—a sharing in God's grace. He is also aware of their love for him, shown in their concern for him during his imprisonment as well as in his ministry of proclaiming the gospel of Christ. They were the first church to send financial aid to him behind bars, and he knew that they were holding him in their prayers.

His longing for them was 'in the compassion of Christ' (v. 8), a rather strange phrase, though not as strange as the King James Version's 'I long for you in the bowels of Christ'! Both are struggling to translate a powerful Greek word that literally means a 'churning of the stomach' and arose from the idea that the seat of our most powerful emotions was down in the digestive system. It is often used of Jesus in the Gospels ('he had compassion on the leper' means that the man's plight 'churned him up'—deeply moved him). That was how Paul's love for the Philippians affected him.

He also prayed that their love (for him, or for Christ?) would issue in 'knowledge and full insight' (v. 9), with the result that they would be able to judge what is for the best and produce a 'harvest of righteousness' (v. 11) in their lives.

Reflection

Paul's affection for the Christians at Philippi, and their loyalty to him, did not exist in order to promote a warm glow! They were gospel virtues for the good of the gospel—and for 'the glory and praise of God'. May our love, too, have that heavenly goal.

DW

Rejoicing in hope

It is my eager expectation and hope that I will not be put to shame in any way, but that by my speaking with all boldness, Christ will be exalted now as always in my body, whether by life or by death. For to me, living is Christ and dying is gain. If I am to live in the flesh, that means fruitful labour for me; and I do not know which I prefer. I am hard pressed between the two: my desire is to depart and be with Christ, for that is far better; but to remain in the flesh is more necessary for you. Since I am convinced of this, I know that I will remain and continue with all of you for your progress and joy in faith, so that I may share abundantly in your boasting in Christ Jesus when I come to you again.

I have chosen these verses for today's reading, but hope that you will read from 1:12–26. Paul, in prison, finds comfort in several factors, all of which may help us when we go through times of trial. Everything that has happened has helped to spread the gospel (v. 12)—the 'whole imperial guard' (v. 13) now knew about Christ. Not only that, but the local Christians had been emboldened by Paul's imprisonment to speak out for Christ (v. 14).

Christ is preached, even by those who do it from wrong motives! Some preach the gospel out of respect for Paul's courage. Some preach it in the hope of getting leading posts in the church after his execution. Never mind, says the apostle. Who cares? Either way, Christ is preached (vv. 15–18)!

If Paul is executed, Christ will be glorified. If he lives, it will be because God has delivered him (v. 19). Not only that, but to die and be with Christ is such a wonderful prospect that Paul is torn between wanting to live and continuing his ministry, or dying and being 'with Christ, for that is far better' (v. 23).

Reflection

Paul's conviction is that God still has work for him to do and that he will 'remain and continue'. When that happens the Philippians will be able to 'boast in Christ Jesus'. It might be helpful to wonder what we feel we could 'boast' about in that way.

DW

The life well lived

Only, live your life in a manner worthy of the gospel of Christ, so that, whether I come and see you or am absent and hear about you, I will know that you are standing firm in one spirit, striving side by side with one mind for the faith of the gospel, and are in no way intimidated by your opponents. For them this is evidence of their destruction, but of your salvation. And this is God's doing. For he has graciously granted you the privilege not only of believing in Christ, but of suffering for him as well—since you are having the same struggle that you saw I had and now hear that I still have.

I like the 'only', though as we read on it becomes clear that Paul knows it isn't simple at all, living life 'in a manner worthy of the gospel of Christ' (v. 27). That would presumably mean living how Jesus lived: a sacrificial life of love and service for others, a total commitment to honesty and a willingness to confront evil wherever it confronts us.

The apostle adds two more concerns of Christ to that list. He is concerned that the Philippian Christians should be completely united. This is in line with the prayer of Jesus that his disciples should 'all be one' (John 17:21). They are also to 'stand firm' and, as Jesus did, fearlessly face evil when it expresses itself in human terms.

Paul's stay in Philippi was hardly an easy one, even though it had such fruitful results. He was attacked by a mob, beaten up by the police and then thrown into the town jail (Acts 16:22–24). Now, it would seem, the Christians there are also under some kind of attack of a similar nature ('the same struggle', v. 30) and so can enter into that 'privilege' of suffering for Christ (v. 29).

There are many Christians who are also experiencing suffering in the name of Jesus. I wonder if we, in the sheltered Western world, feel deprived of a similar blessing?

Reflection

To 'live your life in a manner worthy of the gospel of Christ' is the greatest challenge facing the Christian disciple. It is also the most effective agent of mission, because it is the Christ-like life that draws people to him—'walking the walk' rather than 'talking the talk'.

DW

Christ high exalted

Let the same mind be in you that was in Christ Jesus, who, though he was in the form of God, did not regard equality with God as something to be exploited, but emptied himself, taking the form of a slave, being born in human likeness. And being found in human form, he humbled himself and became obedient to the point of death—even death on a cross. Therefore God also highly exalted him and gave him the name that is above every name, so that at the name of Jesus every knee should bend, in heaven and on earth and under the earth, and every tongue should confess that Jesus Christ is Lord, to the glory of God the Father.

This magnificent 'hymn' (probably a form of words recited or sung in the churches of the time) is quoted by Paul in the context of a call to the Philippians to be united, humble, compassionate and loving (vv. 1–4). They should cultivate the mind of Christ, who voluntarily surrendered 'equality with God' (v. 5) in order to share our human nature. In fact, although his nature (*morphe* in Greek) was divine, he adopted the nature (*morphe*) of a human slave. That is the mystery of the incarnation, the divine expressed in human nature.

The hymn charts the path of the Son of God to the depths of human suffering, not simply death but 'death on a cross' (v. 8) as a criminal, the most shameful death there could be. At that point, however, the word 'therefore' (v. 9) signals a reverse journey. The Son of God, having plumbed the depths of human experience, now begins a journey back to the heights of heaven. He is raised by God from death, 'highly exalted' to his Father's right hand, and given by God 'the name above every name'. That name is 'Jesus'—saviour, deliverer, rescuer. At that name, by which he was once called by his mother from the dusty streets of Nazareth as a boy, 'every knee' in heaven and on earth shall one day bow, confessing that Jesus is both Messiah and Lord—to the glory of God the Father' (v. 11).

Reflection

May the mind of Christ my Saviour
live in me from day to day,
By his love and power controlling
all I do and say.

Kate B. Wilkinson (1859–1928)
DW

Shining like stars

Therefore, my beloved, just as you have always obeyed me, not only in my presence, but much more now in my absence, work out your own salvation with fear and trembling; for it is God who is at work in you, enabling you both to will and to work for his good pleasure. Do all things without murmuring and arguing, so that you may be blameless and innocent, children of God without blemish in the midst of a crooked and perverse generation, in which you shine like stars in the world. It is by your holding fast to the word of life that I can boast on the day of Christ that I did not run in vain or labour in vain.

The word 'therefore' is important, because it links these words of encouragement and gentle warning to the example of Jesus, which immediately preceded it. He left heaven to take on human nature, accepted the role of a servant—and even of a criminal—in order to achieve his Father's purposes. Now, says Paul, apply that to your own situation at Philippi. Wouldn't it be a contradiction of your calling if your church was known as a centre of 'murmuring and arguing'?

So, just as when I was with you, so now in my absence, he argues, 'work out' your 'salvation' (v. 12)—your healthy condition as a church of Jesus Christ—because ultimately it is 'God who is at work in you'. If they live like that, they will 'shine like stars' in a dark world (v. 15). They will be true children of God.

When churches, and the Christians who constitute them, are living like that, they will be agents of light, however dark the world around may seem. This echoes the words of Jesus himself: 'let your light shine before others, so that they may see your good works and give glory to your Father in heaven' (Matthew 5:16). The light is not theirs, but the light of Christ, who is 'the light of the world' (John 9:5). They—and we—are simply reflectors.

Reflection

The apostle is proud of the Christians at Philippi because in a world that must have seemed dark and oppressive they still managed to 'shine as lights' by 'holding fast to the word of life'—the gospel word that is life-giving.

DW

Friends and colleagues

I hope in the Lord Jesus to send Timothy to you soon, so that I may be cheered by news of you. I have no one like him who will be genuinely concerned for your welfare. All of them are seeking their own interests, not those of Jesus Christ. But Timothy's worth you know, how like a son with a father he has served with me in the work of the gospel. I hope therefore to send him as soon as I see how things go with me; and I trust in the Lord that I will also come soon. Still, I think it necessary to send to you Epaphroditus—my brother and co-worker and fellow soldier, your messenger and minister to my need... Welcome him then in the Lord with all joy, and honour such people, because he came close to death for the work of Christ, risking his life to make up for those services that you could not give me.

The whole of the passage is worth reading for its insight into the life of the early Church, with the apostles and their deputies travelling enormous distances to encourage, teach and evangelize. It seems from verse 27 that Epaphroditus had been very ill. He was already known to the Philippians, who had been anxious to hear of his recovery. Paul also indicates that he hoped to be able to visit them shortly—provided he could get out of prison!

The lasting significance of these words, however, is in their warmth and pastoral concern and the picture they paint of what we would now call 'teamwork'. We can see how Paul described Epaphroditus: 'my brother, co-worker and fellow soldier, your messenger and minister to my needs' (v. 25). A 'brother' speaks of a personal relationship; a 'co-worker' makes the apostle and his assistant equals in the task; a 'fellow soldier' tells us that they were in a battle together—presumably against evil and darkness. But Epaphroditus is also a bearer of the same gospel message as Paul, and, perhaps most touchingly, he 'ministers' to the great apostle's needs, even 'risking his life' to do it (v. 30).

Sunday reflection

'Friends and colleagues' is the picture that emerges of the church at Philippi and its itinerant ministers. In Christian service, is it ever possible to be one without also being the other?

DW

Losses and gains

If anyone else has reason to be confident in the flesh, I have more: circumcised on the eighth day, a member of the people of Israel, of the tribe of Benjamin, a Hebrew born of Hebrews; as to the law, a Pharisee; as to zeal, a persecutor of the church; as to righteousness under the law, blameless. Yet whatever gains I had, these I have come to regard as loss because of Christ. More than that, I regard everything as loss because of the surpassing value of knowing Christ Jesus my Lord.

The Philippians, like many other churches at that time, were coming under pressure from the 'Judaizers', people who saw Christianity as a Jewish sect and wanted its adherents to observe the legal and dietary requirements of Judaism. Paul saw such people as obsessed with 'the flesh', whereas the true believer worships 'in the Spirit of God' (v. 3). He then launches into a spirited analysis of his own gains and losses when he turned from being a slave of the 'Law' to being a slave of Jesus Christ.

First, he tots up the 'gains' of his former position. By birth he was a Jew of Jewish parents, circumcised, a member of the people of Israel, of the tribe of Benjamin. By choice he was a Pharisee and a zealous persecutor of the followers of Jesus, Oh, and for a bonus, 'as to righteousness under the law, blameless' (v. 6). What he is saying, in effect, is—if you're going to be a Jew, be a proper one, like me!

Yet—and notice the little word that starts verse 7—all this was less than nothing, compared with 'knowing Christ Jesus my Lord'. For that Paul was prepared to sacrifice everything else. In fact, he rated the things in his past life as 'rubbish', mere refuse (v. 8). The whole of this passage is couched in terms of gains and losses, and Paul is in no shadow of a doubt that his former life of legal, religious observance was 'loss' and that his present life of faith in Christ is all 'gain'.

Reflection

If you or I did a similar exercise to this one of Paul's, how would our 'gains' and 'losses' go? Would scrupulous attention to the detail of religious ritual seem preferable to (or perhaps easier than) the unpredictable business of following Jesus?

DW

Pressing on

I want to know Christ and the power of his resurrection and the sharing of his sufferings by becoming like him in his death, if some-how I may attain the resurrection from the dead. Not that I have already obtained this or have already reached the goal; but I press on to make it my own, because Christ Jesus has made me his own. Beloved, I do not consider that I have made it my own; but this one thing I do: forgetting what lies behind and straining forward to what lies ahead, I press on toward the goal for the prize of the heavenly call of God in Christ Jesus.

Ambition is a funny thing. When I was at school I very much wanted to be a journalist or writer, but 'wanting' wasn't enough to make me do the things necessary to achieve the goal. I wasted time right through to the sixth form and spent the next few years trying to catch up. Still, I did get there, about ten years after leaving school!

Having a wish is one thing, but achieving a goal is another. That's what Paul is talking about here, using his own experience to challenge his friends at Philippi to turn even their spiritual wants and ambitions into genuine goals and then go for them.

He, and probably they, wanted to 'know Christ' (v. 10), to enter into a personal relationship with the Saviour. To achieve that demanded the payment of a cost—not in keeping laws or observing rituals, but in getting priorities right. To know 'the power of his resurrection' we must also share in his sufferings. If we become 'like him in his death'—living a life of self-sacrifice and then offering it to God—then we may attain the res-urrection from the dead.

Paul doesn't think he has already attained all this, but his priority is clear—he forgets what lies behind (not always easy to do) and strains forward to the ultimate goal. And what is that? The prize of being called to heaven by God.

Reflection

To run a good race the athlete must close his or her mind to past failures and simply concentrate on the distant tape, the final goal. That is the one thing that really matters in the end.

DW

The heavenly citizens

Brothers and sisters, join in imitating me, and observe those who live according to the example you have in us. For many live as enemies of the cross of Christ; I have often told you of them, and now I tell you even with tears. Their end is destruction; their god is the belly; and their glory is in their shame; their minds are set on earthly things. But our citizenship is in heaven, and it is from there that we are expecting a Saviour, the Lord Jesus Christ. He will transform the body of our humiliation that it may be conformed to the body of his glory, by the power that also enables him to make all things subject to himself.

As Paul is dictating this letter, some warning light must have flashed in his mind. This church was not riven with dissension; nor was it a hotbed of heresy. Yet for the second time (compare 3:2) he strikes a warning note. Perhaps he was aware how active the Judaizing party were elsewhere in the Church; or perhaps he has in mind Gentile Christians who think that once the soul is saved the body can do what it likes. At any rate, he inserts some powerful sentences of warning! The Philippians should follow Paul's example, and that of their other teachers—but only because Paul himself was following the example of Christ (1 Corinthians 11:1). It was all a question of 'walking', the literal meaning of the verb he uses here. They should 'walk' the way he walked, not the way these 'enemies of the cross of Christ' walked (vv. 17, 18).

In fact, while these (anonymous) false disciples set their minds on earthly things (v. 19), the true believers set theirs on heaven. That is the country where they are really to be 'at home'. It is from heaven that Jesus will return to complete their salvation, transforming not only their inner spirits but also their outward bodies to be like his own.

Reflection

The 'Judaizers' felt that minute observance of ceremony and law were essential to salvation, while some of the Gentiles believed the opposite— that Christians had been freed by Christ to do what they liked. Paul sets the same standard before them both—the message that saved them in the beginning. Go on as you began, he says.

DW

The peace of God

Therefore, my brothers and sisters, whom I love and long for, my joy and crown, stand firm in the Lord in this way, my beloved. I urge Euodia and I urge Syntyche to be of the same mind in the Lord. Yes, and I ask you also, my loyal companion, help these women, for they have struggled beside me in the work of the gospel, together with Clement and the rest of my co-workers, whose names are in the book of life. Rejoice in the Lord always; again I will say, Rejoice. Let your gentleness be known to everyone. The Lord is near. Do not worry about anything, but in everything by prayer and supplication with thanksgiving let your requests be made known to God. And the peace of God, which surpasses all understanding, will guard your hearts and your minds in Christ Jesus.

This passage really needs to be read in its entirety, because the lovely promises about rejoicing and peace are set in the context of a genuine falling-out between Christian friends and co-workers.

Paul couldn't have couched his rebuke of the two women, Euodia and Syntyche, in gentler terms. They were among his 'loved and longed for' brothers and sisters at Philippi (v. 1). They were 'beloved'. They had 'struggled beside him in the work of the gospel' (v. 3)— which suggests that they did more than make the coffee! All of this made it even more painful that they had fallen out with each other. The phrase 'be of the same mind' seems to refer back to 2:5, where the Philippians were urged to 'let the same mind be in them as was in Christ Jesus'—a 'mind' of humble, self-sacrificing service, certainly not operating on the basis of 'selfish ambition or conceit' (2:3). So perhaps Euodia and Syntyche were caught up in some kind of an argument about status. If so, they wouldn't be the first or last in Church history.

On the contrary, they should 'rejoice in the Lord' (v. 4), practise 'gentleness' (v. 5) to everyone (the word could be translated 'graciousness') and replace 'worry' with prayer and thanksgiving (v. 6). When they are doing that, the peace of God will post a guard around their hearts and minds.

Reflection

To 'rejoice in the Lord' is to rejoice as a member of the Lord's family. We belong to him.

DW

Godly content

Finally, beloved, whatever is true, whatever is honourable, whatever is just, whatever is pure, whatever is pleasing, whatever is commendable, if there is any excellence and if there is anything worthy of praise, think about these things. Keep on doing the things that you have learned and received and heard and seen in me, and the God of peace will be with you. I rejoice in the Lord greatly that now at last you have revived your concern for me... Not that I am referring to being in need; for I have learned to be content with whatever I have. I know what it is to have little, and I know what it is to have plenty. In any and all circumstances I have learned the secret of being well-fed and of going hungry, of having plenty and of being in need. I can do all things through him who strengthens me.

The call to 'think about these things' (v. 8) picks up the earlier theme of having the 'mind of Christ'. Indeed, Paul frequently makes the case that it is right thinking that leads to right action (and wrong thinking that has the opposite effect). To discipline their thought life, the Philippian Christians should concentrate on honourable, just, pure, pleasing, praiseworthy things. Every day for 20 years on my way to work at Broadcasting House in London I passed beneath these words, carved in marble and written in Latin, in the entrance hall of the building. It was the prayer of the first BBC governors that such should be the content of the corporation's output. Oh dear!

If the Philippians guarded their thoughts and held faithfully to what Paul and others had taught them, the 'God of peace' would be with them—the play on words with the 'peace of God' (vv. 7, 9) is clearly intentional.

Paul now speaks about himself. Even under detention, he is still able to 'rejoice' (v. 10)—partly because they have sent him a gift, it seems. Not, he hastens to add, because he is in need, but because he had learnt the secret of contentment. The key words then follow: 'I can do all things through him who strengthens me' (v. 13).

Reflection

We do not live in a contented generation! All the more reason, then, for Christians to resist the endless desire for more and better and bigger.

DW

Riches and needs

I have been paid in full and have more than enough; I am fully satisfied, now that I have received from Epaphroditus the gifts you sent, a fragrant offering, a sacrifice acceptable and pleasing to God. And my God will fully satisfy every need of yours according to his riches in glory in Christ Jesus. To our God and Father be glory forever and ever. Amen. Greet every saint in Christ Jesus. The friends who are with me greet you. All the saints greet you, especially those of the emperor's household. The grace of the Lord Jesus Christ be with your spirit.

It would seem that only the church at Philippi had been able to support Paul financially and, consequently, none of the others had received the 'profit that accumulates to your account' (v. 17)—one of several commercial terms that he introduces, probably playfully, into this closing section. Christians giving, in other words, is a two-way thing. We give, but we also receive. More than that, God will 'fully satisfy every need of yours according to his riches in glory in Christ Jesus' (v. 19). All their needs will be met by God—and not just 'met', but gloriously satisfied in a way appropriate to 'God's riches'. These 'riches' are 'in Christ Jesus', a rather strange wording, but consistent with the emphasis of this letter on the glory of the risen and ascended Lord (2:9–11).

As usual, the letter ends with various greetings and benedictions. On this occasion few names are mentioned, probably because the believers with Paul during his captivity were mostly servants of the imperial court, who would be at serious risk if their allegiance to Christ became public. If, as is generally assumed, this letter was written from Ephesus then the 'imperial household' would be a 'government house' for civil servants and Roman officials, something for which there is inscriptional evidence.

The letter ends with a benediction that is very typical of Paul: 'the grace of the Lord Jesus Christ be with your spirit' (v. 23). It is 'grace' which he wants to celebrate, the undeserved yet freely given gift of God in his Son.

Reflection

Paul calls their gifts to him 'a sacrifice acceptable and pleasing to God' (v. 18). What a transforming effect it would have on our gifts for God's work if we could see them in that way!

DW

Tender words

Comfort, O comfort my people, says your God. Speak tenderly to Jerusalem, and cry to her that she has served her term, that her penalty is paid, that she has received from the Lord's hand double for all her sins. A voice cries out: 'In the wilderness prepare the way of the Lord, make straight in the desert a highway for our God. Every valley shall be lifted up, and every mountain and hill be made low; the uneven ground shall become level, and the rough places a plain. Then the glory of the Lord shall be revealed, and all people shall see it together, for the mouth of the Lord has spoken.'

Whenever I see a new motorway being built, I think of this passage. The planning, clearing and levelling that has to take place before a highway is usable often makes the most appalling mess, but it is the only way to achieve that smooth and easily travelled surface.

Isaiah has prophesied judgment, punishment and exile for the people of God—a complete mess. Now, however, he is told to speak tenderly and to comfort them, to tell them what will happen when the time of their punishment is over, and the journey back to their own land begins. He is to promise comfort for the exiles and the forgiveness of sins. The people of God would be living in a foreign land, which would feel to them like a wilderness. As Moses found, however, it is often in the desert that the way back to God is found and the glory of the Lord is revealed.

John the Baptist quoted this passage when he came to prepare the way for the ministry of Jesus. He went out to the wilderness and called people from all walks of life to build the road and begin to travel back to God. No matter where you find yourself today, you can know God's comfort and encouragement and, because 'the mouth of the Lord has spoken', you can be sure that the glory of the Lord will be revealed.

Sunday prayer

Father, thank you for your words of comfort. Thank you that you will one day reveal your glory to all the world. Help me build the road to make that happen.

JO

What shall I cry?

A voice says, 'Cry out!' And I said, 'What shall I cry?' All people are grass, their constancy is like the flower of the field. The grass withers, the flower fades, when the breath of the Lord blows upon it; surely the people are grass. The grass withers, the flower fades, but the word of our God will stand forever. Get you up to a high mountain, O Zion, herald of good tidings; lift up your voice with strength, O Jerusalem, herald of good tidings, lift it up, do not fear; say to the cities of Judah, 'Here is your God!' See, the Lord God comes with might, and his arm rules for him; his reward is with him, and his recompense before him. He will feed his flock like a shepherd; he will gather the lambs in his arms, and carry them in his bosom, and gently lead the mother sheep.

So, says the prophet, what am I to say to a people condemned to exile? At first sight the message seems lacking in comfort—in terms of eternity we spend a very short time on earth, and then we die—a message that is repeated in a biblical version of italics. It is only the word of the Lord that stands forever.

Then Isaiah gives his rallying call. With another repetition he urges the people of God to become a 'herald of good tidings'. They are called upon to proclaim that God is their God. He exists, and he is coming to save.

We, too, are called upon to proclaim the same truth, both to the Church and to the world. The message is that God is coming as judge and ruler to recompense men and women for the way they have lived.

The message is also that he comes as our shepherd, feeding us and caring for the weak and the vulnerable.

Jesus identified himself as the Good Shepherd in John chapter 10. Spend a few minutes reading through that passage and ask him to show you new truths from it. Then look for opportunities to 'cry out' those truths to others today.

Prayer

Father, thank you that your word stands for ever, and that your promise to 'feed your flock' is true for me today.

JO

No comparison

Who has measured the waters in the hollow of his hand and marked off the heavens with a span, enclosed the dust of the earth in a measure, and weighed the mountains in scales and the hills in a balance? Who has directed the spirit of the Lord, or as his counsellor has instructed him? Whom did he consult for his enlightenment, and who taught him the path of justice? Who taught him knowledge, and showed him the way of understanding? Even the nations are like a drop from a bucket, and are accounted as dust on the scales; see he takes up the isles like fine dust, Lebanon would not provide fuel enough, nor are its animals enough for a burnt offering. All the nations are as nothing before him; they are accounted by him as less than nothing and emptiness.

Isaiah was speaking to a people who would be sent into exile. They would live in a foreign land at the mercy of their enemies. Yes, they needed to know that God was their shepherd, but they needed even more to know that he was in charge of their destiny. So the prophet launches into this incredible set of metaphors to show them just who God is. The whole earth to him is like a few particles of dust in scale, and the oceans that cover our planet just a drop in his bucket. He has all power, all knowledge, and everything in the world is not enough to appease his anger.

For us, travel and communication have made the world small. Our weapons can reduce the isles to dust. Our computers can perform incredible calculations in seconds. The very rich are described as 'having more money than God'. Has the culture in which we live relegated God to an optional extra, a comfort blanket in hard times, a supplier of daily bread?

Solomon tells us in Proverbs that the beginning of wisdom is to fear God. Soak your mind today in thoughts of God's power and might, knowledge and authority; learn to fear him and worship him in his majesty.

Prayer

Almighty and all-powerful God, help me to understand that you rule over this world and that no nation, no leader, no organization is outside your control.

JO

An image that will not topple

To whom then will you liken God, or what likeness compare with him? An idol?—A workman casts it, and a goldsmith overlays it with gold, and casts for it silver chains. As a gift one chooses mulberry wood—wood that will not rot—then seeks out a skilled artisan to set up an image that will not topple.

The prophets of the Old Testament always seem to save their most blistering attacks and their most biting sarcasm for the sin of idolatry. Here Isaiah, in his desire to show the people what their God is really like, pauses a moment to consider the futility of idols. To take an image and cover it with gold or to make a very special idol as a present for someone, using wood that will not rot, and fixing it securely to the wall—how can this possibly compare with knowing and worshipping the living God?

There the idol sits, deteriorating in wind and weather, unable to move or speak. Could the people really imagine that this was better than worshipping the creator God, the ruler of the universe and the judge of all? What a joke! Though the land of their exile would be filled with such images, and with those who believed them powerful, God's people are to avoid such folly. Their God is not even like such gods. He is as far above them as the heavens are above the earth.

As human beings we long for stability and security. Something that stays put and remains permanently fixed may perhaps have an attraction for us. God, however, is unpredictable. Jesus told us that if we want to know what God is like, we should look at him; and he was anything but predictable. Did he ever answer a question straightforwardly or heal in the same way twice? Did he not flummox his enemies and often shock his friends?

Don't be tempted to pin God to the wall and overlay him with gold. He will surprise you over and over again and your search for security may be just another form of idolatry.

Prayer

Father, forgive me for Jesus' sake, if I have made an idol and called it my saviour. Surprise me today with your power and your love.

JO

The ruler of princes

Have you not known? Have you not heard? Has it not been told you from the beginning? Have you not understood from the foundations of the earth? It is he who sits above the circle of the earth, and its inhabitants are like grasshoppers; who stretches out the heavens like a curtain, and spreads them like a tent to live in; who brings princes to naught, and makes the rulers of the earth as nothing. Scarcely are they planted, scarcely sown, scarcely has their stem taken root in the earth, when he blows upon them, and they wither, and the tempest carries them off like stubble.

The people who want to know who rules the world are not the political pundits or the voters. It is the refugee, the slave, the prisoner of war—these are the ones with a deep need to know that their life and times are not in the hands of their oppressors, but under the control of a loving Father.

Politicians, kings and queens, dictators and despots all come and go. The iron curtain dividing Europe seemed immovable and eternal, but it has disappeared. The Berlin wall was built strong and high, but it was torn down. The ovens of Auschwitz were real, but the nightmare came to an end.

Who decided the dates of those happenings? Isaiah trumpets to an oppressed and captive people that it is their God—Jahweh—and he alone who rules. To him, the politicians and kings and dictators are no more than the grass in his garden—to be planted and watered and fed, and then to be mown down as he sees fit.

Because we are limited to time and to the moment, we may find it very hard to believe that what is now will not be forever. God, however, is outside time, and for him, the Roman empire, Idi Amin, Saddam Hussein, Hitler and every other ruler who thumbs their nose at him, are as nothing. He allowed them for a while, but in his great purpose for the world their time came to an end.

Let your prayers for the world today be inspired by the knowledge of his ultimate power.

Meditation

'All authority,' said Jesus, 'in heaven and earth has been given to me'
(Matthew 28:17).

JO

Not one is missing

To whom then will you compare me, or who is my equal? says the Holy One. Lift up your eyes on high and see: Who created these? He who brings out their host and numbers them, calling them all by name; because he is great in strength, mighty in power, not one is missing.

'We are all in the gutter, but some of us are looking at the stars,' said Oscar Wilde. The prophet Isaiah agrees! He urges those in the gutter, in exile, in some kind of trouble, to look up at the stars and to consider the one who created them.

The gutter is a lonely and desperate place. It is cold and hard. Those who are there are abandoned by the world and despised by the rich and comfortable. They have lost their place in society, whether temporarily or permanently, and feel an overwhelming sense of being lost and alone.

You may not be homeless in a big city, physically sitting in the gutter and watching the world go by, but perhaps you feel that way spiritually. Does everyone else seem to be totally content, enjoying a rich inner life? Does everyone but you seem to have a place in God's purpose and a job to do for him? Do you feel that, like the people of God, you have lost your place in his kingdom and exist in a kind of grey exile, far from the warmth of his presence?

I tell you, the people of God cannot be lost to him. Isaiah writes that God knows and names every last star in the universe and has never lost a single one of them. The stars of the heavens, the sand on the seashore, the hairs of our head—all are known and numbered by him. We cannot begin to understand such power and knowledge, but what we can do is to rejoice in the fact of it.

Meditation

Read carefully through Psalm 8 for a slightly different angle on the stars! The psalmist felt threatened at first by their remoteness: 'What are human beings, that you are mindful of them…?' Then he draws comfort, just as Isaiah tells us to, from the power of God, and his great love for his creation.

JO

Fly like the eagle

Why do you say, O Jacob, and speak, O Israel, 'My way is hidden from the Lord, and my right is disregarded by my God'? Have you not known? Have you not heard? The Lord is the everlasting God, the Creator of the ends of the earth. He does not faint or grow weary; his understanding is unsearchable. He gives power to the faint, and strengthens the powerless. Even youths will faint and be weary, and the young will fall exhausted; but those who wait for the Lord shall renew their strength, they shall mount up with wings like eagles, they shall run and not be weary, they shall walk and not faint.

We are now three weeks into January—how are your New Year's resolutions? By this time you may have discovered, along with every human being since the fall, that we grow 'weary in doing what is right' (Galatians 6:9). Isaiah knew that the people of God would grow weary in exile; weary of battling against a culture totally opposed to their God.

Maybe to begin with they would believe it possible to ignore the faith system and worldview of those around them, to remain totally in love with Yahweh, trusting his power to save them. But they would grow weary and begin to question whether God was capable of rescuing them, let alone willing to do so.

'What are you talking about?' thunders Isaiah. 'You know perfectly well what God is like! His strength and wisdom are eternal and he will never tire of caring for you and providing for you. Wait for him!'

What does it mean to you, that phrase, 'Wait for the Lord', or as some versions put it, 'Wait on the Lord'? Is it like a child waiting for Christmas—the longing for it to come, the certainty of wonderful things happening, the ticking off of the days? Or does it have connotations of waiting in the sense of serving (see, for example, Psalm 123)?

For those prepared to wait on God, to wait for him to act, the most amazing strength is promised. We are promised strength to fly like an eagle, run a marathon, walk without dropping.

Prayer

Almighty Father, give to all your people, young and old, the strength to go on trusting you and working for you.

JO

27

All one in Christ

When I was asked to write a series on this subject, my immediate thought was, 'But we're not! The Church is riven with conflict, disagreement, schism and antagonism.' Division exists at a local level, a national one and even an international one.

Not only that, but missionaries, in the great era of missionary endeavour, exported the divisions with the gospel they brought. As a result, countries that know nothing of the great East–West divide in 1054 or of Reformation, countries for whom this is foreign history, reproduce the same denominational separations.

So instead of writing on 'all one in Christ', I have found myself, on most days, writing about the things that stop us being united and cause the world to be not a little sceptical when we talk of the love of God.

Why is the Church so divided? Why do some think they're the only ones who've got the truth, while others regard them as 'dangerous fundamentalists'? I've tried to explore this by looking at how even the greatest Christians are still subject to human weakness and deception. Jesus must have known there would be conflict among his followers, or he wouldn't have given instructions for how to handle it.

In the first week, I look at discord between individuals within a congregation and how we can best manage it. On a more hopeful note, I will also look at what Jesus called 'the things that make for peace' (Luke 19:42).

Next month, when we return to this subject, I will be exploring the ever-increasing number of different denominations that the Church has split into over the last millennium or so. There are no denominations in the Bible, but it is surprising how many Bible passages can guide us as we seek to deal with the divisions we have today.

Conflict, and its resolution, is a bit of a 'specialist subject' for Mennonites; so I hope you'll forgive me for mentioning 'the Mennos' more often than usual.

Two significant dates occur during our two sets of readings: Holocaust Memorial Sunday and Women's World Day of Prayer. They both point us to sources of potential unity: unity in suffering and unity in prayer. One will come whether we want it or not, but the other might be a good place to start when we want to be as one.

Veronica Zundel

Jesus' unanswered prayer

[Jesus prayed] 'I ask not only on behalf of these, but also on behalf of those who will believe in me through their word, that they may all be one. As you, Father, are in me and I am in you, may they also be in us, so that the world may believe that you have sent me. The glory that you have given me I have given them, so that they may be one, as we are one, I in them and you in me, that they may become completely one, so that the world may know that you have sent me and have loved them even as you have loved me.'

'I'll pray for you.' What do you think when you hear someone say that? I suspect it largely depends on who is saying it. If it's a trusted friend or church leader, someone you know to be a person with a deep spiritual life, you will draw comfort from their promise. If not, you may just see it as an excuse not to do anything else. (After all, you have perhaps made the same promise often enough and failed to keep it—I have…).

I wonder if it has ever occurred to you that Jesus himself prayed for you? You, me and all who have followed Jesus through the ages—Paul, Augustine, Julian of Norwich, Mother Teresa—are included in the prayer we read today. I don't know about you, but I find that hard to take in!

What is even harder to grasp—but it's true—is that Jesus' prayer here has not (yet) been answered. Jesus' disciples have never been 'completely one… as we are one'

and show few signs of ever being so.

Why? There's no easy answer, except that God has given us free will, the choice to agree or disagree, indeed the choice to follow Jesus or not. God, strange as it may seem, has put the power of answering certain prayers into our hands.

Prayer is not a way of forcing the things you want to happen. Sadly, after 2000 years, Jesus' prayer is still unanswered. Might we have the power to answer it?

Sunday reflection

At church or at home today, think of one small action you could do to make unity in Christ come closer.

VZ

Disputatious disciples

James and John, the sons of Zebedee, came forward to [Jesus] and said to him, 'Teacher, we want you to do for us whatever we ask of you.' And he said to them, 'What is it you want me to do for you?' And they said to him, 'Grant us to sit, one at your right hand and one at your left, in your glory.' But Jesus said to them, 'You do not know what you are asking...' When the ten heard this, they began to be angry with James and John.

Sibling rivalry is not something I've had to deal with as a parent, since my son is an only child! I have watched plenty of other mothers trying to referee disputes between their children, though, and have been called in, or gone in voluntarily, to find out what the raised voices between my son and a friend are all about.

In the case of James and John, it was actually brothers who had got together to plot how to 'get one over' the other disciples. It must have felt to Jesus as if he were the parent of a large, quarrelling family, where everyone was vying for the top place in Mum's or Dad's affections: 'I'm the favourite!' 'No, I am!'

We might think that if Jesus were among us in the flesh, all our disputes of doctrine, practice and just plain old personality clashes would be instantly settled—in fact they wouldn't even arise, we'd be so absorbed in watching and learning from our redeemer.

This story gives the lie to that. Human beings are human beings, however close to Jesus, and we will always have aspirations, opinions and little ways that cause conflict. The twelve disciples were no better than we are, and we are no better than they were.

Perhaps unity in Christ is not a case of whether or not we disagree, but of how we handle disagreement. If our prime motivation is to be right, and be acknowledged to be right, we can never be one. Jesus suggested another way: 'whoever wishes to become great among you must be your servant' (v. 43)

Reflection

'Among the Gentiles... their rulers lord it over them, and their great ones are tyrants over them. But it is not so among you' (vv. 42–43). *Or is it?*

VZ

Divided we fall

Those conflicts and disputes among you, where do they come from? Do they not come from your cravings that are at war within you? You want something and do not have it; so you commit murder. And you covet something and cannot obtain it; so you engage in disputes and conflicts. You do not have, because you do not ask. You ask and do not receive, because you ask wrongly, in order to spend what you get on your pleasures.

Tweedledum and Tweedledee
Agreed to have a battle;
For Tweedledum said Tweedledee
Had spoiled his nice new rattle.

So runs one of the rhymes in Lewis Carroll's *Through the Looking Glass*. It's always seemed to me an admirable summing up of how human quarrels start: with a supposed offence, an accusation and a willingness to fight over it.

James' summary of where human conflict comes from is perhaps less catchy, but equally accurate. If we expect other human beings, or the things around us in the world (which are largely provided by other human beings), to give us 100 per cent of our satisfaction in life, we are likely to come to verbal, if not physical, blows when they don't actually see this as their primary purpose for living. If A wants X and B has it but won't or can't give it to A, then we have a battle on our hands.

The X in question might be something material or it might be 'spend more time with me', or even a desire for your minister to preach a favourite doctrine of yours (which he or she might not agree with).

The solution, James suggests, is that we look for fulfilment not to other people, but to God. That doesn't mean human relationships are unimportant; they are vital. But they will always be imperfect; only God can meet our deepest needs.

Alice's rhyme goes on: 'Just then flew down a monstrous crow / As black as a tar barrel, / Which frightened both our heroes so, / They quite forgot their quarrel.' A common enemy, as was often noted in World War II, unites people very effectively. Just imagine what a common friend might do!

Reflection

In my church, when we cannot agree on an issue, we stop a meeting and have a period of silent meditation. It can be surprisingly unifying.

VZ

Settling out of court

[Jesus said] 'If another member of the church sins against you, go and point out the fault when the two of you are alone. If the member listens to you, you have regained that one. But if you are not listened to, take one or two others along with you, so that every word may be confirmed by the evidence of two or three witnesses. If the member refuses to listen to them, tell it to the church; and if the offender refuses to listen even to the church, let such a one be to you as a Gentile and a tax collector.'

Since the 16th century, this passage has been central for the Anabaptist movement, from which my Mennonite Church sprang. In most other churches of the time, church discipline largely took the form of imprisoning, torturing and killing those who were seen as heretics (including many Anabaptists).

The Anabaptists, however, practised only 'the ban', or excommunication, for those who would not respond to attempts to correct them. It was seen as a non-violent way of dealing with disputes, as opposed to 'the sword' wielded by the state churches. It was meant to lead to reconciliation (which would be impossible if you had burned or beheaded the offender!).

Over the centuries, however, Mennonites and other Anabaptists have abused the ban just as much as other churches abused their power to take life. I wonder whether 'shunning' was really what Jesus meant by 'let such a one be…

as a Gentile and tax collector'. After all, what he did with Gentiles and tax collectors was to eat with them, heal them and generally reach out to them; not avoid them!

Could he perhaps have meant: 'if they are not behaving in a Christian way, regard them as a non-Christian, love them and witness to them'? 'The ban' has sadly led to much disunity among Anabaptist Christians. I have a feeling that Jesus' way, if I'm right about this interpretation, would be much better at promoting unity.

Reflection

'So when you are offering your gift at the altar, if you remember that your brother or sister has something against you, leave your gift there before the altar and go; first be reconciled to your brother or sister, and then come and offer your gift' (Matthew 5:23–24).

VZ

One in the Spirit

If then there is any encouragement in Christ, any consolation from love, any sharing in the Spirit, any compassion and sympathy, make my joy complete: be of the same mind, having the same love, being in full accord and of one mind. Do nothing from selfish ambition or conceit, but in humility regard others as better than yourselves. Let each of you look not to your own interests, but to the interests of others. Let the same mind be in you that was in Christ Jesus...

In George Eliot's early novel *The Mill on the Floss*, there is a publican who deals with disputes in his pub by saying, 'You're both right and you're both wrong, as I always say'. Whatever you think of his fence-sitting, he strikes me as a man who has his priorities right; it is more important to him to promote harmony than to discover who's right.

In Matthew 18, Jesus suggests a procedure for dealing with conflict. Today's passage tells us (as Paul also points out in 1 Corinthians 13) that, without a spirit of love and humility, any amount of correct procedure will be inadequate to create unity.

Our unity as followers of Jesus must be based on the spirit of Jesus; he is the source of our hope, our strength and our understanding of others. If we do not learn and constantly practise these qualities, we will always be riddled with conflict and division.

Where do we learn them? From Jesus himself, to start with; but also, I believe, from those we encounter who are further on than us in the ways of peace. Paul puts it like this: 'Be imitators of me, as I am of Christ' (1 Corinthians 11:1). A recent study by the Evangelical Alliance has spoken of the need for churches to practise 'a culture of apprenticeship' so as to make mature disciples.

I am a slow learner, but I feel I have learnt much over the last 14 years from others in the Mennonite Church about how to be a Christ-like person. For us all to become more like Jesus is ultimately the only way to discover and nurture unity.

Prayer

Pray for anyone in your church with whom you have had conflict or with whom you just don't get on well. Next time you see them, think about how Jesus would approach them.

VZ

This one thing we do

I therefore, the prisoner in the Lord, beg you to lead a life worthy of the calling to which you have been called, with all humility and gentleness, with patience, bearing with one another in love, making every effort to maintain the unity of the Spirit in the bond of peace. There is one body and one Spirit, just as you were called to the one hope of your calling, one Lord, one faith, one baptism, one God and Father of all, who is above all and through all and in all.

Have you ever taken part in one of those group exercises beloved of management trainers, in which you have to build a bridge with cardboard boxes or create a 'human sculpture' on some theme or other?

In my experience, such efforts often disintegrate into long arguments about the best way to do the job and who will do what, so that the task itself gets cobbled together in the last five minutes or not at all.

Paul here pleads with his hearers to keep their eye on the job, which is to serve God and make God known. It's not a question of being purely task-oriented, however, and failing to take into account the feelings of the people involved. Many a church has floundered on thinking that their mission is all, forgetting that this mission can only be achieved by people working well together.

God's task is one that can only be fulfilled by being people-oriented—if the task is to love God and spread God's love, this is completely inseparable from loving each other. The 'two great commandments' (Matthew 22:36–40) are really one commandment, for 'those who do not love a brother or sister whom they have seen, cannot love God whom they have not seen' (1 John 4:20).

In the next section of this study, in about a month, we will be looking at unity—or the lack of it—between different church groups and denominations. There are too many of these to count—but there is only 'one God and Father of all', who is the basis of true unity.

Reflection

*'Who serves my Father as a son
[or daughter]
Is surely kin to me'*

John Oxenham, 'In Christ there is no
east or west' (1908)
VZ

One in joy and sorrow

When the builders laid the foundation of the temple of the Lord, the priests in their vestments were stationed to praise the Lord with trumpets... And all the people responded with a great shout when they praised the Lord, because the foundation of the house of the Lord was laid. But many of the priests and Levites and heads of families, old people who had seen the first house on its foundations, wept with a loud voice when they saw this house, though many shouted aloud for joy, so that the people could not distinguish the sound of the joyful shout from the sound of the people's weeping, for the people shouted so loudly that the sound was heard far away.

Today is Holocaust Memorial Sunday, commemorating the genocide in which my mother's mother, aunt and uncle all perished. It's also two days since the date on which my brother committed suicide over 30 years ago. Though he was born in the UK, I regard him, too, as a victim of the disruption Nazism caused in my parents' lives, leading them to become refugees in a country where they had no extended family to support them.

There are groups campaigning for this day to become a day commemorating all victims of genocide and persecution; a day on which we grieve in solidarity with those who were destroyed by human evil. Suffering can be a great force for unity—though one wouldn't want to seek it out!

In today's passage, however, the people are divided between those who grieve and those who celebrate, according to their life experiences. Yet in a mysterious way they are still united, because everyone's experience and mood is accepted as valid.

Our churches are likely at any time to have some who are sorrowing and some who are full of joy. We are told in Romans 12:15 to 'rejoice with those who rejoice, weep with those who weep'. This is a challenge to those of us who lead or preach—unless we can learn to do both, we risk alienating one or another of our group. Unity comes from listening to both the tears and the laughter.

Reflection

'A friend loves at all times, and kinsfolk are born to share adversity' (Proverbs 17:17). When has your church—or your family—been most united?

VZ

Prayer in Luke's Gospel

The traditional symbol for Luke the evangelist in much Christian art and iconography is the ox—the patient bearer of burdens throughout much of the ancient world. Luke does indeed show Christ as the bearer of burdens. In the synagogue at Nazareth, he set out the programme for his ministry in those famous words from the prophet Isaiah—to work for the poor, the captives, the blind and the oppressed, in the knowledge and power of God's calling to him (4:16–21).

It may seem that in focusing simply on prayer in Luke's Gospel, this crucial aspect is being overlooked. It is true that it is rather in the background in this fortnight's readings, although not absent altogether. On the other hand, prayer is shown by Luke as one of Jesus' main resources for bearing the burden of this ministry. It is all connected.

Luke, in fact, has a strong emphasis on prayer; he shows Jesus at prayer nine times in all, nearly as many as the eleven times found in the other three Gospels put together. To balance this private prayer, his entire Gospel has as its 'bookends' corporate worship in the temple in Jerusalem.

Prayer is not only to build Jesus up in his ministry, however. It is also a place in which he discovers and strengthens his relationship with God, his Father, and in which he prays for his disciples. Through seeing him at prayer, his disciples want to share in it, and so they ask him to teach them to pray, too. He shares with them what we now call the Lord's prayer, the pattern of prayer for all Christians, and teaches them to enter into the same relationship with God that he himself enjoys.

About half of the material in Luke's Gospel is not found in the other three Gospels, and among the original material are three vivid parables about prayer—the friend at midnight, the unjust judge and the Pharisee and the tax collector praying in the temple. Luke's Jesus is very concerned for the spiritual life of his disciples, teaching them that they must trust God to fulfil their needs just as a good parent does, to persevere in prayer, and to throw themselves on God's mercy. These are gifts just as much needed for the work of social justice, which is the other passion of Luke's Gospel.

Helen Julian CSF

Son of Joseph, Son of God

Now when all the people were baptized, and when Jesus also had been baptized and was praying, the heaven was opened, and the Holy Spirit descended upon him in bodily form like a dove. And a voice came from heaven, 'You are my Son, the Beloved; with you I am well pleased.' Jesus was about thirty years old when he began his work. He was the son (as was thought) of Joseph son of Heli... son of Enos, son of Seth, son of Adam, son of God.

It is a very familiar story. It's easy to rush on to the climax, the marvellous words that confirm the identity of Jesus, and so miss the significance of the context in which this affirmation happened.

Jesus had been baptized, along with 'all the people', identifying himself with his people, God's people, the people of Israel. Immediately after this momentous event, he is praying. This way of telling the story is found only in Luke. In both Mark and Matthew, the voice is heard as Jesus comes up out of the water (Mark 1:10–11; Matthew 3:16–17). It's an early sign (though not the first) of the importance of prayer and worship in Luke's Gospel.

One of the purposes of prayer in this Gospel is thus introduced too. It may be a rather unexpected one; we are familiar with prayer of thanksgiving, of intercession, of penitence, but here we have prayer as a means of establishing and confirming identity. It is in prayer,

in the context of baptism, that Jesus, according to Luke, first hears himself called 'Son'—and not just Son, but also Beloved.

The words that Jesus hears are drawn from two different places in the Old Testament. First, there is Psalm 2:7, which describes the king who will establish God's reign, and then Isaiah 42:1, where we read about the servant of God, in whom God delights. So in these few words we already have a multiplicity of echoes and a richness of identity.

When we are unsure of our identity we can follow Jesus' example and turn to God in prayer, knowing that he will speak to us as he did to Jesus.

Sunday reflection

As we begin this study of prayer in Luke's Gospel, reflect on what part prayer plays in your life.

HJ CSF

Choosing with God

Now during those days [Jesus] went out to the mountain to pray; and he spent the night in prayer to God. And when day came, he called his disciples and chose twelve of them, whom he also named apostles: Simon, whom he named Peter, and his brother Andrew, and James, and John, and Philip, and Bartholomew, and Matthew, and Thomas, and James son of Alphaeus, and Simon, who was called the Zealot, and Judas son of James, and Judas Iscariot, who became a traitor.

What do you do when you need to make an important decision? Perhaps you draw up lists of all the factors, dividing them into 'for' and 'against', or go to see a trusted friend and talk it all over with them.

Jesus here is at an important point in his ministry. He is going around teaching and healing and many are being drawn to follow him, but many are also critical of how he seems to be breaking the rules that they value. Just before this passage there are several stories of conflict with the Pharisees, especially about what it was lawful to do on the Sabbath. Jesus needs to gather his own support around him. But whom should he choose, out of all those who are following him?

For Luke the context of most of the major events of Christ's life—his baptism, the confession of Peter, the transfiguration, the betrayal—is prayer. So the choosing of the twelve apostles is preceded by a night of solitary prayer. Mark and Matthew have stories of the choosing of the apostles (with some different names—for the Gospel writers the number twelve, which matches the twelve tribes of Israel, is more important than the exact names)—but neither mentions Jesus praying before making his choice.

We need to be aware that making prayer part of our decision-making doesn't guarantee that everything will go smoothly as a result. It didn't work that way for Jesus. Those he chose didn't always understand who he was or learn quickly what he was trying to teach them. One of them even became a traitor.

Prayer for discernment will help to ensure that our choices are informed by God, but God ultimately leaves us free to make those choices.

Reflection

How do you involve God in your choices?

HJ CSF

Rhythms of life

Once, when [Jesus] was in one of the cities, there was a man covered with leprosy. When he saw Jesus, he bowed with his face to the ground and begged him, 'Lord, if you choose, you can make me clean.' Then Jesus stretched out his hand, touched him, and said, 'I do choose. Be made clean.' Immediately the leprosy left him... But now more than ever the word about Jesus spread abroad; many crowds would gather to hear him and to be cured of their diseases. But he would withdraw to deserted places and pray.

It wasn't only in times of crisis or decision that Jesus turned to prayer. In this brief story we have an indication of a regular habit: 'he would withdraw... and pray'. He stepped back from all the demands of his ministry, from the crowds who came to hear him preach and to ask for healing, to spend time alone with God.

For Luke this was an essential element of Jesus' ministry. In fact it underpinned it all. Denis McBride comments on this passage: 'And as the people seek after Jesus, he seeks after his Father, so that he can be immersed in the power which makes healing and the future possible' (*The Gospel of Luke: A reflective commentary*, Dominican Publications, 1991, p. 74).

Perhaps this makes prayer sound quite functional. Jesus became tired by the demands of the crowds, and needed to get away, to have some space. Perhaps this was a part of it; he was, after all, human as well as divine, and must have become wearied by his work at times. Yet prayer had a much deeper purpose than this.

As we have already seen in the story of the baptism, it was in prayer that he heard the words 'you are my Son', and we can assume that this building up of relationship with his Father continued. We can also assume that he took the needs of the people with him to the deserted places and into his prayer.

The rhythm of activity and prayer that Jesus models is an important one for us, and his commitment to prayer in the midst of so many demands is an inspiration for us.

Reflection

What priority do you give prayer in your life? What do you see as its purpose for you?

HJ CSF

Challenging prayer

Once when Jesus was praying alone, with only the disciples near him, he asked them, 'Who do the crowds say that I am?' They answered, 'John the Baptist; but others, Elijah; and still others, that one of the ancient prophets has arisen.' He said to them, 'But who do you say that I am?' Peter answered, 'The Messiah of God.' He sternly ordered and commanded them not to tell anyone, saying, 'The Son of Man must undergo great suffering, and be rejected by the elders, chief priests, and scribes, and be killed, and on the third day be raised.'

Jesus knew who he was; his hours in prayer had revealed it to him, and confirmed him in it. Now, out of a time of prayer—prayer alone and yet not quite alone—come two key questions for them and for us:

'Who do people, who does the world, say that I am?' There were then, as there are now, many different answers to that question. For the people of Jesus' time, the answers come in the form they are familiar with, that of the prophets of the Old Testament. For our time and people and place the answers may be couched in terms more familiar to us—a great teacher, a good man.

'But who do you say that I am?' Now the question becomes personal and has to be answered out of our own hearts and minds. No one else can answer this question for us.

Peter answers that he is the one long awaited, the king sent to usher in God's rule. This recognition sparks off in Jesus further revelation. Now that he has been acknowledged, he teaches his disciples what this identity means. It isn't what they would have expected. The expectation was that the Messiah would come in power, but he speaks of suffering, rejection and death. Then he goes on in the following verses to say that his followers will share the same fate—they must take up their cross and be prepared to lose their lives for his sake.

Out of prayer come challenging questions, and revelations of identity and of vocation, which will change the lives of the disciples.

Prayer

Jesus, make me open to hear your questions to me and help me to answer them from my heart.

HJ CSF

Rejoicing in simplicity

At that same hour Jesus rejoiced in the Holy Spirit and said, 'I thank you, Father, Lord of heaven and earth, because you have hidden these things from the wise and the intelligent and have revealed them to infants; yes, Father, for such was your gracious will. All things have been handed over to me by my Father; and no one knows who the Son is except the Father, or who the Father is except the Son and anyone to whom the Son chooses to reveal him.'

So far, we have seen Jesus at prayer, but have not shared the content of that prayer. Here we have some words, and, characteristically for Luke, they are words of praise and joy.

Jesus has sent his disciples out in pairs to prepare the way for him, and they have returned joyfully with marvellous stories of God's work through them. This prayer is Jesus' response. The 'infants' are the disciples—they are still young and unformed in faith, but God has done his work through them. The kingdom is open to those who will enter it in the simplicity of infants, not to those who want to 'think themselves in'. Jesus gives thanks for the way in which everything is being turned upside down in the coming of the kingdom.

The Holy Spirit plays an important role in Luke's Gospel—in fact the Spirit initiates each section of the Gospel. We saw how the Spirit descending as a dove marked the beginning of Jesus' public min-istry; here the Spirit appears at the beginning of the journey to Jerusalem.

In his prayer Jesus is continuing to explore his identity. There is a deepening here of his sense of uniqueness as the only Son of the Father. This relationship is not meant for himself alone; he can and does reveal the Father to those whom he chooses and can draw them to share in something of the same relationship, as God's beloved children.

This is a deeply trinitarian passage and shows the relational character of the Trinity. Denis McBride describes it poetically: 'Jesus is the Word between the silence of God and the understanding in the Spirit' (*The Gospel of Luke,* p. 137).

Prayer
Threefold God, reveal yourself to me, as I come to you in simplicity.

HJ CSF

Salvation for all people

Now there was a man in Jerusalem whose name was Simeon; this man was righteous and devout, looking forward to the consolation of Israel, and the Holy Spirit rested on him. It had been revealed to him by the Holy Spirit that he would not see death before he had seen the Lord's Messiah. Guided by the Spirit, Simeon came into the temple; and when the parents brought in the child Jesus, to do for him what was customary under the law, Simeon took him in his arms and praised God, saying, 'Master, now you are dismissing your servant in peace, according to your word; for my eyes have seen your salvation, which you have prepared in the presence of all peoples.

The Holy Spirit inaugurates Jesus' public ministry; the Spirit was also powerfully present at the very beginning of his life.

Elizabeth is promised that her son, John the Baptist, will be filled before his birth with the Spirit; Mary is told that she will conceive the Messiah by the power of the Spirit; Elizabeth recognizes who Mary is carrying in her womb through the Spirit; Zechariah prophesies by the power of the Holy Spirit. Now the Spirit rests on Simeon and guides him to go to the temple and to speak his own prophecy about this wonderful child. Where Zechariah gave thanks for the redemption of his own people, Simeon has a wider vision, praising God for coming to save 'all peoples'.

Praise is an important element of prayer in Luke's Gospel; it begins with the three songs of praise and prophecy of Mary, Zechariah and Simeon, two of them in the temple in Jerusalem, and ends back in the temple, where the disciples are described as 'continually... blessing God' (24:53).

Today in many churches Simeon's recognition of Jesus as the Messiah, for whom he had waited all his life, will be celebrated in the feast of Candlemas. 'The consolation of Israel' was one of the ways in which the rabbis described the coming age of the Messiah (the phrase comes from the opening of Isaiah 40), but Simeon sees beyond this expectation, great as it was, and includes us, the Gentiles, in his praise and blessing.

Prayer

Light of the world, fill me with praise as I see your salvation.

HJ CSF

God with us

As [Jesus] approached the gate of the town, a man who had died was being carried out. He was his mother's only son, and she was a widow... When the Lord saw her, he had compassion for her... Then he came forward and touched the bier... And he said, 'Young man, I say to you, rise!' The dead man sat up and began to speak, and Jesus gave him to his mother. Fear seized all of them; and they glorified God, saying, 'A great prophet has risen among us!' and 'God has looked favourably on his people!'

In this story of the raising of the widow's son at Nain, there are echoes of many of the themes we have already considered. Jesus' identity is a source of speculation, and some are sure that he is a great prophet. There are deliberate parallels with the story of Elijah and the widow of Zarephath (1 Kings 17:8–24), which ends with Elijah raising her son from the dead, and the widow proclaiming Elijah to be a man of God.

Here, too, Jesus is recognized as a prophet, but in the words 'God has looked favourably on his people' some are perhaps reaching towards something more. 'Looked favourably' may remind us of the Magnificat, where Mary rejoices that God has 'looked with favour' on his servant (Luke 1:48). Tom Wright writes that 'looked favourably' means 'God has come near to us, to save and rescue us' (*Luke for Everyone*, SPCK, 2004, p. 84). Of course God comes near in his prophets, but much nearer in his Son.

Luke certainly gives a hint of this in the words he uses. For the first time in his Gospel Jesus is called 'Lord' and is shown as Lord of both the living and the dead.

Another of Luke's themes also appears in this story—his concern for the poor and the needy. A widow with only one son was already in a very vulnerable position, and once he had died she was left entirely alone, with no one to protect her in a very male-dominated society. Jesus' compassion for her plight is characteristic of his care for those who are powerless—children, the elderly and women.

Prayer

Lord, give me your compassion for those in need and prayer like yours, powerful to help.

HJ CSF

Learning to pray

[Jesus] was praying in a certain place, and after he had finished, one of his disciples said to him, 'Lord, teach us to pray, as John taught his disciples.' He said to them, 'When you pray, say: "Father, hallowed be your name. Your kingdom come. Give us each day our daily bread. And forgive us our sins, for we ourselves forgive everyone indebted to us. And do not bring us to the time of trial."'

There are two versions of the Lord's prayer in the Gospels—this one and Matthew's (6:9–13). Matthew's is longer, but it seems likely that the original version was somewhere between the two versions. In my opinion, however, Luke's context was probably the original one—the disciples, inspired by Jesus' example of prayer, asked him to teach them to pray with the same intimacy and all-encompassing trust of God.

Jesus gives them this very simple pattern of prayer. From the very first word, he draws them into the same relationship with God that he himself enjoys, telling them to address God as Father. Famously, he uses the familiar child's word *Abba* rather than the formal religious term *Abinu*. Whichever word is used, he is, in using the term 'Father' to address God, also placing the disciples with him as God's children and hence looking back to the God of the exodus, who could say that Israel was his 'firstborn son' (Exodus 4:22).

As God in the exodus had given his people all they needed in their journey through the wilderness, so the disciples can bring all of life into their prayer. They can pray for the coming of the kingdom, for the revelation of God's purposes on earth, and in the next breath pray for their daily bread, that their very basic need for sustenance will, day by day, be satisfied.

They can pray for their relationships with one another, that forgiveness may be at the heart of their common life, and for God's protection against everything that may harm them and their relationship with him. In these five petitions there is enough material for a lifetime's prayer.

Sunday reflection

Could your prayer life be an inspiration to others? If someone said to you 'teach me to pray', where would you start? How is prayer taught in the life of your church?

HJ CSF

Persistent prayer

[Jesus said] 'So I say to you, Ask, and it will be given you; search, and you will find; knock, and the door will be opened for you. For everyone who asks receives, and everyone who searches finds, and for everyone who knocks, the door will be opened. Is there anyone among you who, if your child asks for a fish, will give a snake instead of a fish? Or if the child asks for an egg, will give a scorpion? If you then, who are evil, know how to give good gifts to your children, how much more will the heavenly Father give the Holy Spirit to those who ask him!'

Luke, with his particular interest in prayer, has three parables on prayer found nowhere else in the Gospels, and this teaching follows one of them, the story of the friend coming at midnight to beg for bread (you will find the others in 18:1–8 and 9–14). This story and the one of the widow and the unjust judge press home the same message, that of persistence as a virtue in prayer—what Tom Wright calls 'a holy boldness'.

Persistence may seem a double-edged recommendation, with God cast in the role of the reluctant neighbour or the unjust judge, having to be nagged into giving what we want and finally succumbing to stop us bothering him. But this teaching counteracts that image. If our parents on earth are generous and caring to us their children, how much more, says Jesus, will our heavenly Father give generously to all those who ask. As one commentator remarks, this is not the theology of the insurance company, 'in which acts of God are understood only in terms of disaster' (Denis McBride, *The Gospel of Luke*, p. 147).

Luke again stresses the importance of the Holy Spirit in Jesus' ministry, by replacing Matthew's 'good things' in his parallel passage (Matthew 7:7–11) with the promise of the Holy Spirit. Prayer is the context in which this gift is given, and it is also a gift for prayer and for ministry, as we see in Luke's second book, Acts (see, for example, Acts 2 and 7:1–18).

Prayer

Father, make me persistent in prayer and strengthen me with the gift of your Holy Spirit.

HJ CSF

Looking to God

[Jesus] also told this parable to some who trusted in themselves that they were righteous and regarded others with contempt: 'Two men went up to the temple to pray, one a Pharisee and the other a tax collector. The Pharisee, standing by himself, was praying thus, "God, I thank you that I am not like other people: thieves, rogues, adulterers, or even like this tax collector. I fast twice a week; I give a tenth of all my income." But the tax collector, standing far off, would not even look up to heaven, but was beating his breast and saying, "God, be merciful to me, a sinner." I tell you, this man went down to his home justified rather than the other; for all who exalt themselves will be humbled, but all who humble themselves will be exalted.'

The third of Luke's unique parables of prayer has a more cautionary lesson for us. Being people of prayer does not guarantee God's favour, and we can use prayer to play games with God and with each other just as we can use many other things.

The key difference between the Pharisee and the tax collector is where they are looking when they pray. The Pharisee is looking at himself and at other people and comparing himself favourably to them. Although he was in fact doing far more than the law required, which was fasting just once a year, and giving a tenth of certain kinds of income, he was putting his trust in his own virtue rather than in God's mercy and using his 'catalogue of negative virtues and minor pieties' (G.B. Caird, *Saint Luke*, Penguin, 1963, p. 202) to exalt himself.

The tax collector is looking first to God and seeing himself in the light of God's infinite holiness and goodness and thus perceiving his own condition far more clearly. He sees that his only hope lies in God's goodness and so throws himself on God's mercy.

That is what God requires above all. Our sinfulness need not keep us from God if we look past it to him, and our virtue will not bring us nearer to God if we allow it to stand between us and him.

Prayer
Gracious God, keep my eyes fixed on you and not on myself.

HJ CSF

He prays for us

[Jesus said] 'You are those who have stood by me in my trials; and I confer on you, just as my Father has conferred on me, a kingdom, so that you may eat and drink at my table in my kingdom, and you will sit on thrones judging the twelve tribes of Israel. Simon, Simon, listen! Satan has demanded to sift all of you like wheat, but I have prayed for you that your own faith may not fail; and you, when once you have turned back, strengthen your brothers.'

Today we begin to see more intimately Jesus' own prayer. It's the feast of the Passover; Jesus has celebrated the last supper with his disciples, and foretold his own death and suffering. Despite all this, they are still arguing about who is the greatest. Jesus overturns their assumptions by telling them they must be like him and that he is among them 'as one who serves' (v. 27)

Part of his service has been to pray for them, especially when their faith is being tested. Surely this must have been a regular part of his prayer from the day he chose them? So much rested on them, and they seemed so ill-equipped for the task. In his times of solitary prayer, away from the crowd, the needs of his disciples must often have been presented to his Father.

We also get a hint in this story of Jesus' own wrestling with an awareness of the powers ranged against him. However we understand 'Satan' we cannot doubt that there is evil in the world, opposing what is good and of God, and that some do fall away and cease to follow the living God. Jesus cannot prevent the struggle from happening, but he can stand with those who are being tested, adding his powerful prayer to their petition to be saved from 'the time of trial' (11:4).

God has made a covenant with Jesus ('confer' carries this sense), and in turn Jesus makes a covenant with his disciples and, through them, with his whole Church, both then and now. We can be assured that if we remain within 'the kingdom', then Jesus will be praying for us in our times of trial, as he was for Simon Peter.

Reflection

In difficult times, see Jesus joining his prayer with yours and be strengthened.

HJ CSF

The weapon of prayer

[Jesus] came out and went, as was his custom, to the Mount of Olives; and the disciples followed him. When he reached the place, he said to them, 'Pray that you may not come into the time of trial.' Then he withdrew from them about a stone's throw, knelt down, and prayed, 'Father, if you are willing, remove this cup from me; yet, not my will but yours be done.'… When he got up from prayer, he came to the disciples and found them sleeping because of grief, and he said to them, 'Why are you sleeping? Get up and pray that you may not come into the time of trial.'

Luke's is the only Gospel in which Jesus invites his disciples to join in his prayer in the garden of Gethsemane, perhaps a sign of the centrality of prayer in Luke's vision of the Christian life. As Jesus joins his prayer with our prayers, so we are invited, like the disciples, to join our prayers with his. Sometimes this may be in joyful praise of God, but at other times it will be in the anguish of Jesus' prayer in the garden, as he wrestled with what seemed to be God's will, but from which his whole being recoiled.

Recoiling at the prospect of his own imminent suffering and death, he wondered if he should accept the cup that God held out to him. Perhaps he also recoiled at the prospect of entrusting the cause of the kingdom to a group of disciples who seemed to have grasped so little during his time with them. Would all his work go to waste and his death be pointless?

No wonder that this anguished prayer drove him to his knees, although the normal Jewish position for prayer was standing.

Prayer is the only weapon that Jesus teaches his disciples to use. They want to use the weapons of war when the crowd comes to arrest Jesus (v. 49), but Jesus will have none of it (v. 51). Prayer to the Father is the only thing that will enable them to move through their fear and sorrow and enter the relationship of love and trust with the Father in which Jesus is still acting.

Prayer

In my times of trial, O Father, let me use only the weapon of prayer.

HJ CSF

Trusting to the end

It was now about noon, and darkness came over the whole land until three in the afternoon, while the sun's light failed; and the curtain of the temple was torn in two. Then Jesus, crying with a loud voice, said, 'Father, into your hands I commend my spirit.' Having said this, he breathed his last. When the centurion saw what had taken place, he praised God and said, 'Certainly this man was innocent.'

This relationship of love and trust is to be tested yet further through the dreadful events of Jesus' passion and death. The whole of creation is shaken as he dies on the cross. The natural explanation for the sun's light failing is that an eclipse took place, but in fact it is impossible to have a solar eclipse at the time of the full moon, and the feast of the Passover always took place at full moon.

For the original readers of the Gospel, this impossible event would have strengthened their sense of the crucial importance of what was happening on Good Friday. Important events were often accompanied by portents (see Amos 8:9; Joel 2:10, 31; 3:15). Jesus would, of course, have been aware of this part of his religious tradition.

Jesus' final prayer, his final words of love and trust to his loving and trustworthy Father, are taken from Psalm 31:5, another part of his tradition, this time of worship. Psalm 31 was tradition-ally used as part of Jewish night prayer and so, as this unnatural night fell around the cross, Jesus turned to the familiar words, consciously committing himself to his Father. The psalm begins, 'In you, O Lord, I seek refuge… in your righteousness deliver me' and perhaps Jesus' ability to pray this psalm in his agony was the fruit of a lifetime of faithful prayer in all circumstances.

Even in his death his prayer made an impact on others, as it had on his disciples when they asked to be taught to pray. As the centurion saw the calm and trusting way in which Jesus died, he was moved to praise God. Perhaps he, too, came in the fullness of time to learn to pray as Jesus did, and to enjoy the same relationship with the Father.

Prayer

God of refuge, let me trust in you, in life and in death.

HJ CSF

Companion in prayer

Now on that same day two of them were going to a village called Emmaus... While they were talking and discussing, Jesus himself came near and went with them, but their eyes were kept from recognizing him... As they came near the village... he walked ahead as if he were going on. But they urged him strongly, saying, 'Stay with us, because it is almost evening and the day is now nearly over.' So he went in to stay with them. When he was at the table with them, he took bread, blessed and broke it, and gave it to them. Then their eyes were opened, and they recognized him; and he vanished from their sight.

The much-loved story of the disciples on the road to Emmaus will, of course, remind many of us of the Eucharist, and it is a powerful image of how Jesus comes to us in that sacrament. It should also take us back to other meals that Jesus shared with his friends. The disciples who met him on their journey had not been at the last supper and must therefore have recognized the gesture of taking and breaking bread from some of those other meals.

There are in fact seven other significant meals in Luke's Gospel, beginning with the feast given by Levi after his conversion and call, and so this is the eighth. Eight was a number of fulfilment, the day beyond the seventh and final day of creation, and so a sign of new creation. This meal is a token of the heavenly banquet.

This story also has more to teach us about prayer as we come to the end of our journey through Luke's Gospel. It shows us how powerful the prayer of blessing can be; it is in Jesus' blessing of the bread that the two disciples come to recognize him. It is a marvellous image of those brief but powerful glimpses of Jesus that can come to us in unexpected times and places, in our prayer as in our worship, relationship, study and struggle. It provides us with a picture of Jesus walking with us even when we don't recognize him—a powerful and consoling idea when prayer seems dry and dark.

Prayer

Jesus of the Emmaus road, walk with me in word and sacrament.

HJ CSF

Grace abounding

Teenagers can be cruel. Brothers can be cruel to their elder brothers—and vice versa, of course. As a teenager, my elder brother had a girlfriend; her name was Grace. Suddenly the youth group became surprisingly enthusiastic about choosing hymns and choruses. They could be seen avidly scouring the book searching for their favourite—and curiously all their favourites had one biblical concept in common: grace. It had a charming sound, but not one particularly harmonious to my brother's ear, confused as it was by the childish giggles around the room. I remember the episode to this day. What I also remember is that the concept of grace had inspired a remarkable number of hymn writers—it really was a case of grace abounding.

John Bunyan, the 17th-century tinker who became a preacher imprisoned for his faith, wrote his autobiography and called it 'Grace Abounding to the Chief of Sinners'. He saw God's grace at work as God patiently drew him to faith despite all his failings and false starts. He was acutely aware of his sin and therefore acutely aware of just how undeserving of God's love he was.

It was the same thought that inspired the slave-trader turned hymn writer John Newton, who described himself as a 'wretch' and had just two words to describe the fact that God had rescued him and given him new life: Amazing Grace.

I wonder if you say 'grace' before you eat a meal. It is an opportunity to recognize that all we have is a gift from God; it's an opportunity to say thank you. The Greek word translated 'grace'—*charis*—captures this link. Sometimes it emphasizes the gift, sometimes the thankfulness for the gift. That thankfulness is expressed by our willingness to multiply the grace by our own generosity. It's beautifully expressed in Henry Smith's simple song: the weak and the poor blessed because God has blessed us.

Give thanks with a grateful heart
Give thanks unto the Holy One
Give thanks because He's given
Jesus Christ, His Son

And now let the weak say,
'I am strong'
Let the poor say, 'I am rich'
Because of what the Lord has done
for us. Give thanks.

Or as American writer Jackie Windspear put it: 'Grace isn't a little prayer you chant before receiving a meal. It's a way to live.'

Stephen Rand

51

Gracious, good to all

I will exalt you, my God the King; I will praise your name for ever and ever. Every day I will praise you and extol your name for ever and ever. Great is the Lord and most worthy of praise; his greatness no one can fathom. One generation will commend your works to another; they will tell of your mighty acts. They will speak of the glorious splendour of your majesty, and I will meditate on your wonderful works... The Lord is gracious and compassionate, slow to anger and rich in love. The Lord is good to all; he has compassion on all he has made. All you have made will praise you, O Lord; your saints will extol you.

What makes you want to worship God? What gets you out of bed on a Sunday morning to sing God's praises?

David was inspired to burst into song by God's greatness, by all that he had done—his mighty acts and his wonderful works. But there was more. David recognized that these stemmed from God's very character; his 'wonderful works' reflected his nature, they were the inevitable result of his 'gracious compassion'.

Notice how the psalm rhymes ideas: 'gracious and compassionate' is immediately followed by a mirror image: 'slow to anger and rich in love'. David could see that by all rights God could treat the world with the wrath and judgment that people's constant sin and rebellion deserved. Yet he was— and is—slow to anger, gracious.

That gracious goodness extends to all. God is not selective—he has compassion on *all* he has made'. This is 'common grace'—common in that it is shared by all equally; uncommon in its breadth and in its glory. God upholds the universe every moment by his power; so every moment of life is an expression of his love.

So as you worship God today, remember all he has done for you; recognize that this stems from and reveals his character; acknowledge that you have done nothing to deserve it. Praise God that this grace is the common experience of all.

Sunday prayer

Loving Father, thank you that you do not treat us as we deserve. Thank you that your goodness is experienced by all. Help us all to recognize you in the daily blessings we receive from your hand. Amen

SR

The sunrise of grace

[Jesus said] 'You have heard that it was said, "Love your neighbour and hate your enemy." But I tell you, love your enemies and pray for those who persecute you, that you may be children of your Father in heaven. He causes his sun to rise on the evil and the good, and sends rain on the righteous and the unrighteous. If you love those who love you, what reward will you get? Are not even the tax collectors doing that? And if you greet only your own people, what are you doing more than others? Do not even pagans do that? Be perfect, therefore, as your heavenly Father is perfect.'

Here, at the heart of the Sermon on the Mount, Jesus states very clearly the principle of 'common grace'. Sunshine and rain, the two vital sustainers of life, are provided by God without distinction, for good and bad alike. This is indeed 'grace abounding'. It is universal, across time and space.

For Jesus this is not simply a theological truth to be stated and admired, however. It is a reality that reveals the character of God and therefore the character of the disciple. Part of God's perfection is the truth that he loves and cares for all, for the entire human race. Thus part of the perfection demanded of his followers is that they too love and care for all, including their enemies.

It is an uncomfortable challenge. Each of us has to think how it might apply to us. Perhaps our hospitality is legendary—but does Jesus really mean we should invite our enemies into our homes?

Wasn't he simply using overstatement, hyperbole, to make his point?

It might certainly mean being pleased rather than offended when the gay couple, the asylum-seeker or the group of noisy teenagers choose our church. It might mean being as willing to have them round for dinner as well as those who are more 'like us'.

Churches expend lots of energy and time on pastoral care of their members. God's example of common grace challenges us to expend the same for our non-members.

Reflection

As we consider what this challenge might mean for us, remember in prayer those in the persecuted church who wrestle with the challenge of loving those who have killed their pastors and destroyed their churches.

SR

Grace for a second chance

I sank down to the bottom of the mountains. I thought I had died and gone down into the grave forever. But you brought my life up from the very edge of the pit. You are the Lord my God. When my life was nearly over, I remembered you, Lord. My prayer rose up to you. It reached you in your holy temple in heaven. Some people worship the worthless statues of their gods. They turn away from the grace you want to give them. But I will sacrifice a thank offering to you. And I will sing a song of thanks. I will do what I have promised. Lord, you are the one who saves.'

I love telling the story of Jonah! The trouble is, it is usually in the 'children's slot' on a Sunday morning, just before they are liberated to go and really enjoy themselves. There is evidence that adults remember a good children's talk more than even the best sermon…

God chooses Jonah for a vital task. A whole city needs to hear of God's love, and Jonah is the man for the job. So does he set out on the road to Nineveh? No, he catches a boat in the opposite direction. Then he discovers that disobeying God can bring disaster—and he is tipped into the sea, only to be swallowed by a great fish.

In the darkness and desperation, he does what you might do—he prays. As our passage (from the New International Reader's Version) demonstrates, he prays with surprising eloquence and insight. At the heart of his prayer he acknowledges that the big problem with worshipping statues is that they are not famous for giving their followers a second chance. Yet even before Jonah knows his fate he embraces the God who saves the undeserving, who does give a second chance.

What's more, Jonah takes his second chance. His message brings the whole city to repentance. Then he is upset because Nineveh has been given a second chance! For them he wanted the wrath of God rather than the grace that had rescued him. How hard it can be to treat others as God has treated us!

Prayer

Lord, help me to take your offer of a second chance—and rejoice when you do the same for others. Amen

SR

The promise of God's word

As the rain and the snow come down from heaven, and do not return to it without watering the earth and making it bud and flourish, so that it yields seed for the sower and bread for the eater, so is my word that goes out from my mouth: It will not return to me empty, but will accomplish what I desire and achieve the purpose for which I sent it. You will go out in joy and be led forth in peace; the mountains and hills will burst into song before you, and all the trees of the field will clap their hands.

What do baptism, Communion, marriage and preaching have in common? Various branches of the Church regard them, not without occasional controversy, as being 'means of grace'. They are all ways in which we can receive from God, of knowing his presence, of building relationship with the Almighty.

Today's verses are the inspiration and the encouragement all preachers need. Not because *their* words will set the hills singing and the trees bursting into wild applause; the promise is that if the preacher releases God's word, God will use it and bless it. God's word created the universe; he spoke and it was done. God's word is powerful—and God's word is for you.

So many find it difficult to receive from God. They can't believe that God would bother with them. They can't accept that he is as gracious as all that—but he is. Even when you read these few verses each day God can speak to you, can come to you, can bless you. They can be a means of grace to you.

Do you remember the story of Josiah? In 2 Kings 23 you can read how he became king of Judah at the age of eight and, 18 years later, part of the written word of God was rediscovered in the temple. Josiah read it, obeyed it—and it became a means of grace, so that Jeremiah could say, 'He did what was right and just, so all went well with him. He defended the cause of the poor and needy, and so all went well' (Jeremiah 22:15–16).

Prayer

Dear Lord, as we read your word each day, graciously give us each day our daily bread. Feed us and sustain us we pray. Amen

SR

Spiritual sustenance

[Jesus said]: 'Do not work for food that spoils, but for food that endures to eternal life, which the Son of Man will give you... I tell you the truth, it is not Moses who has given you the bread from heaven, but it is my Father who gives you the true bread from heaven. For the bread of God is he who comes down from heaven and gives life to the world.' 'Sir,' they said, 'from now on give us this bread.' Then Jesus declared, 'I am the bread of life. He who comes to me will never go hungry, and he who believes in me will never be thirsty.'

Isn't it strange how those things that are most precious can be the source of so much argument? The Communion service is a 'means of grace'—but the apostle Paul had to castigate the Corinthian church about their abuse of the service, Christians have almost literally fought wars about it, and deciding who can take it and who can't has caused grief to countless numbers down the years.

So let's concentrate on what should unite Christians everywhere—it is first of all about Jesus. 'Do this in remembrance of me', he said (Luke 22:19). As we break the bread to remember his life and the broken body of his death, we remember the one who said 'I am the bread of life'. The truth is, we can't live without him.

Jesus can come to us in all sorts of ways; we couldn't restrict him even if we wanted to. He certainly can come to us as we take the bread of Communion. It helps us to focus on him, to open our lives to him, prompting us to receive spiritually as we receive physically. How tragic if it became just an empty ritual, a religious ceremony without personal involvement and spiritual reality.

One way to avoid that tragedy is to recognize that Jesus' body was broken so that a new body could be put together—the Church, which is the body of Christ. We receive God's grace in Jesus not just individually but corporately. Our Communion with Jesus is also a Communion with his followers.

Prayer

Almighty God, teach us what it truly means to feed on you in our hearts by faith with thanksgiving. Amen

SR

Grace and truth

The Word became flesh and made his dwelling among us. We have seen his glory, the glory of the One and Only, who came from the Father, full of grace and truth. John testifies concerning him. He cries out, saying, 'This was he of whom I said, "He who comes after me has surpassed me because he was before me."' From the fullness of his grace we have all received one blessing after another. For the law was given through Moses; grace and truth came through Jesus Christ. No one has ever seen God, but God the One and Only, who is at the Father's side, has made him known.

Fullness is a glorious word. It bursts with that sense of generosity, of wholeness, of completeness that is characteristic of God and the way he deals with people. There is nothing here that is penny-pinching, grudging or abstemious. Part of the glory that John saw was the glory of generosity expressed in the grace of God in Jesus.

It is a source that is constantly and instantly replenished. As we receive one blessing after another, the store is never diminished. Grace is never out of stock, never in short supply. Jesus is never stretched thin as a result of being in great demand. God made his Son available to the world, and he is still available, in all his fullness, to all.

Jesus was full of grace and truth; grace and truth came through him. Grace and truth are a magnificent combination. Christians sometimes have a remarkable ability to be so concerned about truth that they lose all their grace. Relationships are broken over minutiae of biblical interpretation; the media delight in hard-faced and hard-hearted Christian spokespeople who will denounce fellow Christians with enormous enthusiasm.

Jesus was—and is—the truth. He spoke the truth. He was—and is—uncomfortable for this very reason. At the very moment that he forces us to confront the reality about ourselves he is offering himself, his life, to each one of us in the light of that reality. He knows all about us—and loves us just the same. That's glorious.

Prayer
Loving, gracious Lord, fill us with the knowledge of your truth and your Spirit of grace to speak it and live it to the full, so that we give glory to you. Amen

SR

Evidence of grace

Now those who had been scattered by the persecution in connection with Stephen travelled as far as Phoenicia, Cyprus and Antioch, telling the message only to Jews. Some of them, however, men from Cyprus and Cyrene, went to Antioch and began to speak to Greeks also, telling them the good news about the Lord Jesus. The Lord's hand was with them, and a great number of people believed and turned to the Lord. News of this reached the ears of the church at Jerusalem, and they sent Barnabas to Antioch. When he arrived and saw the evidence of the grace of God, he was glad and encouraged them all to remain true to the Lord with all their hearts.

You have just read this passage today because of the story it tells. You stand in the line of countless millions who are the inheritors of the actions of unnamed men from Cyprus and Cyrene. You have become part of the evidence of the grace of God that Barnabas first saw in action in Antioch.

The first Christians were Jewish. Both inside and outside the church the Jesus party were seen as a subgroup within Judaism. They talked of Jesus as the Messiah, the fulfilment of God's promise to the Jews. It is hard for us to imagine just how unthinkable it was that non-Jews might be in the least bit interested in Jesus.

So the situation needed lateral thinking. It needed divine inspiration. It needed people to go against their cultural and religious prejudices and practices. Peter, of course, needed a vision of animals being lowered in a sheet to change his mind (Acts 10:9–16). Above all it needed the grace of God for his message of new life in Jesus to break all the barriers of race, creed, tradition and prejudice, simply because God is for everyone and refuses to be confined to anyone's small box of restrictions.

Rejoice that God is like that, because Gentiles, people like us, were once firmly on the outside; but now we can become one of the family.

Reflection

Barnabas was the great encourager. How encouraged are you when you see evidence of the grace of God as the outsiders of society become welcomed into God's family? How much do you share that encouragement with others?

SR

A story of grace

[Ruth] exclaimed, 'Why have I found such favour in your eyes that you notice me—a foreigner?' Boaz replied, 'I've been told all about what you have done for your mother-in-law... how you left your father and mother and your homeland and came to live with a people you did not know before... May you be richly rewarded by the Lord, the God of Israel, under whose wings you have come to take refuge.' 'May I continue to find favour in your eyes, my lord,' she said. 'You have given me comfort and have spoken kindly to your servant—though I do not have the standing of one of your servant girls.' At mealtime Boaz... offered her some roasted grain. She ate all she wanted and had some left over.

The story of Ruth is a beautiful illustration of God's grace. First, it is reflected in the action of Ruth insisting that she should accompany her mother-in-law on her journey back to Bethlehem. This is the grace that takes risks for the sake of others.

Then Ruth, a foreigner, is welcomed and cared for by the people of God. This is the grace revealed in the law God gave to Moses, which insisted that widows and foreigners should receive special care and consideration, because of their vulnerability, because they had no access to the land that provided food for each day.

So Ruth was entitled to glean in the fields so as not to go short of food, but Boaz then takes over—and goes beyond the requirement of the law in his generosity in providing for Ruth and Naomi: grace revealed in practical action.

The book of Ruth begins with famine and ends with fullness. That's exactly how God's grace works. The prodigal son returned and went from slops to ox roast. God's promise to us is that he will be all that we need—and there will still be plenty of him left over for others. Ruth came from the outside and became part of the family—indeed, part of the family tree that links Abraham to Jesus, by way of David.

Sunday prayer

Today, Lord Jesus, help us to find even more of the fullness of your grace—in our worship, in our hunger for you and your word, in our sharing of your blessings with those on the outside. Amen

SR

Enriched by grace

Grace and peace to you from God our Father and the Lord Jesus Christ. I always thank God for you because of his grace given you in Christ Jesus. For in him you have been enriched in every way—in all your speaking and in all your knowledge—because our testimony about Christ was confirmed in you. Therefore you do not lack any spiritual gift as you eagerly wait for our Lord Jesus Christ to be revealed. He will keep you strong to the end, so that you will be blameless on the day of our Lord Jesus Christ. God, who has called you into fellowship with his Son Jesus Christ our Lord, is faithful.

The apostle Paul begins his letter to this church—which was causing him such grief—by not only wishing them more of God's grace and peace, but also acknowledging that for all their excesses, all their immaturity, all their misplaced enthusiasm, all their moral failings, they had been enriched by God's grace.

Perhaps sometimes we need to be reminded that just as we can't earn our place in God's kingdom, neither can we earn God's blessing in our lives for him. He doesn't bless us because we deserve it; he blesses us because that's the kind of gracious God he is.

This enrichment is not financial, it's spiritual. Their knowledge of God and his word has been expanded and God has poured out his gifts of grace. While they did not merit this, they did desire it. It was their hunger for God that released the flow of his grace and enriched their lives.

The Lord's 'grace is sufficient' (2 Corinthians 12:9). Not only were their lives being enriched right now, but they would also be kept strong and presented blameless before God, so they could enjoy fellowship with him forever. Just as at any and every moment God's grace can never be stretched too thin, so between now and the end of time it will never run out. It is inexhaustible. We receive it, we are enriched by it, we bless others because of it, and we thank God.

Prayer

Gracious God, grant us a hunger to receive from you and the longing to use your gifts with the same grace that has given them. For Jesus' sake. Amen

SR

ROMANS 12:4–8 (TNIV)

Gifts of grace

For just as each of us has one body with many members, and these members do not all have the same function, so in Christ we, though many, form one body, and each member belongs to all the others. We have different gifts, according to the grace given us. If your gift is prophesying, then prophesy in accordance with your faith; if it is serving, then serve; if it is teaching, then teach; if it is encouraging, then give encouragement; if it is giving, then give generously; if it is to lead, do it diligently; if it is to show mercy, do it cheerfully.

On a recent Sunday at my church, the service had just finished, and the worship group were making their way to the door past our visiting preacher. Suddenly he turned to one of them and said, 'You have a beautiful voice; you really helped me into the presence of God this morning.' I was deeply impressed. When I have preached, I wait for others to encourage me; this man was ready with encouragement for another. What a gift!

The week before, one of our leaders had encouraged the congregation to be ready to prophesy if they sensed God had something to say, and three people did. Afterwards a young man came up to one of them and said 'What you shared was the final piece of encouragement I needed. Now I'm ready to be baptized.'

It is not always like that! But that's what God intends. From his grace he gives gifts—not to split the Church into charismatics and non-charismatics, but to encourage, to build up, to allow people to contribute and people to receive. Some Christians worry about the strange and the supernatural and miss the simple and straightforward. The list of gifts is packed with things we all do, simple and straightforward things that under God can make a huge difference.

A gift returned unopened can't bless anybody. A gift received and used is a gift to the whole Church and multiplies the grace with which it was given. In my case, when a poor sermon produces a good response, I know God's grace has been at work!

Prayer

Lord, thank you for your gifts. Help me to use mine and to enjoy the expressions of the gifts of others.
Amen

SR

ROMANS 5:20—6:23 (NIV, ABRIDGED)

Sin defeated

Where sin increased, grace increased all the more, so that, just as sin reigned in death, so also grace might reign through righteousness to bring eternal life through Jesus Christ our Lord. What shall we say, then? Shall we go on sinning, so that grace may increase? By no means! ... For we know that our old self was crucified with him so that the body of sin might be done away with, that we should no longer be slaves to sin... For sin shall not be your master, because you are not under law, but under grace... now that you have been set free from sin... the benefit you reap leads to holiness, and the result is eternal life. For the wages of sin is death, but the gift of God is eternal life in Christ Jesus our Lord.

God will not be beaten. No matter how much sin and wickedness there may be in the world, it cannot overcome God's willingness to be generous. No matter how desperate the human condition, God is ready with his gift. And it is the ultimate gift, absolutely no expense spared. It is the gift of eternal life, bought for us by Jesus through his death on the cross.

The cross of Jesus does not just make it possible for us to know eternal life; it established a whole new order, one characterized not by law but by grace. No longer weighed down by our failure to meet God's demands, but now set free to live in the way God intended.

God's grace is not to be cheapened by sordid calculation, though. If we are ready to test God's generosity by presuming up-

on his willingness to forgive as an invitation to selfish indulgence, then we have missed the point. God's grace brings new life, and that new life is as eternal as the just reward for sin is final. It is a life lived under a new master, the one who has defeated the enemy who was in control.

So many Christians live in the past—a past of failings and legalism. The present is to be lived in the light of the future, receiving the gift of eternal life and living in the benefit of it—now.

Prayer

Thanks be to God for his indescribable gift!

SR

Sharing God's grace

Above all, love each other deeply, because love covers over a multitude of sins. Offer hospitality to one another without grumbling. Each of you should use whatever gift you have received to serve others, faithfully administering God's grace in its various forms. If you speak, you should do it as those who speak the very words of God. If you serve, you should do it with the strength God provides, so that in all things God may be praised through Jesus Christ. To him be the glory and the power for ever and ever. Amen.

Have you noticed how often we contrast the spiritual and the practical? Yet we should always do the practical things with spiritual insight and the spiritual things with practical effectiveness. Paul identified administration as a spiritual gift, given to the Church as an expression of God's grace. Here Peter wants God's grace to be administered faithfully.

Actually the Greek word used is often translated 'steward'. Just as God gave the whole earth to human beings to care for on his behalf, so he continues to give gifts that are to be used, not for our own ends, but in the service of others. It's not just about doing things decently and in order; it's about reflecting the generosity of God in the way we use his gifts.

What could be more practical than a collection for famine relief? However, as Paul considers how Christians should give—he calls it an act of grace—he is provoked into the most glorious description of God's grace, the model for our own behaviour: 'For you know the grace of our Lord Jesus Christ, that though he was rich, yet for your sakes he became poor, so that you through his poverty might become rich' (2 Corinthians 8:9).

Whether that wealth is financial, spiritual, emotional, intellectual—it is a gift from God, given to be shared. A family starving because of the injustice of international debt are fed as a result of the generosity of God's people; an asylum-seeker fleeing for her life is welcomed and housed by a church—this is the love that covers a multitude of sins.

Prayer

God, grant your Church administrators who are accurate in detail and bold to do your will, so that in every way your love can be received and shared with others. Amen

SR

Saved for a purpose

But because of his great love for us, God, who is rich in mercy, made us alive with Christ even when we were dead in transgressions—it is by grace you have been saved. And God raised us up with Christ and seated us with him in the heavenly realms in Christ Jesus, in order that in the coming ages he might show the incomparable riches of his grace, expressed in his kindness to us in Christ Jesus. For it is by grace you have been saved, through faith—and this not from yourselves, it is the gift of God—not by works, so that no one can boast. For we are God's workmanship, created in Christ Jesus to do good works, which God prepared in advance for us to do.

Every Christian once was dead and now is alive—God is in the resurrection business! It must be grace—how could anyone dead possibly be able to earn God's mercy? Because it is God's grace, this is not a penny-pinching 'no more than is necessary' kind of deal. Instead, we are raised to the highest place, the best seat in the cosmos, right next to Jesus in all his glory.

Why? So that the whole creation can see what God is like, the incomparable riches of his grace. So that we can know God's love and be saved from his righteous judgment. So that we can be set free from death and live life to the full—now and for eternity. So that—as Paul emphasizes here—we can fulfil God's purpose in our lives.

Too many Christians think salvation is an end in itself. God intends it to be a doorway to sharing his work, serving him by serving others, working and walking the way God always intended. This is the best possible reason to get out of bed in the mornings! God did not and does not simply rescue us from death; he makes life worth living, because our lives—and what we do with them—have eternal value.

Reflection

If we are God's workmanship, we can be sure that the master craftsman of creation will do a good job. While we can't earn salvation by our good deeds, they must be a confirmation of God's grace at work in our lives.

SR

The throne of grace

Therefore, since we have a great high priest who has gone through the heavens, Jesus the Son of God, let us hold firmly to the faith we profess. For we do not have a high priest who is unable to sympathize with our weaknesses, but we have one who has been tempted in every way, just as we are—yet was without sin. Let us then approach the throne of grace with confidence, so that we may receive mercy and find grace to help us in our time of need.

This is the wonder of Jesus—he has brought God to us, and he brings us to God. He brought the heavenly to earth; he takes the earthly into the heavens. He has walked the glorious vistas of paradise; he has trodden the dusty byways of human habitations. As Paul wrote, 'Though he was rich, yet for your sakes he became poor' (2 Corinthians 8:9) and '[He] did not consider equality with God something to be grasped, but made himself nothing, taking the very nature of a servant, being made in human likeness. And being found in appearance as a man, he humbled himself and became obedient to death—even death on a cross! Therefore God exalted him to the highest place…' (Philippians 2:6–9).

That highest place is a throne of grace. It is the source of blessing, coming from one who has demonstrated that power can be laid aside and the authority that comes from sacrifice can take its place.

So no longer does the subject cringe with fear before the might of majesty. Esther waited at the door of the king, knowing he had the power of life and death over her. We can approach the King of Kings with confidence—Jesus, our high priest, has made representations on our behalf. We are accepted as children of the king. Children can bring the biggest problems and the slightest worry to their father. Grace not only gives the confidence to approach, but the confidence that we will not come away empty-handed.

Prayer

*We echo Paul's prayer for the church in Corinth (2 Corinthians 13:14):
'May the grace of the Lord Jesus Christ, and the love of God, and the fellowship of the Holy Spirit be with you all.' Amen*

SR

The breaking point

After some days Paul said to Barnabas, 'Come, let us return and visit the believers in every city where we proclaimed the word of the Lord and see how they are doing.' Barnabas wanted to take with them John called Mark. But Paul decided not to take with them one who had deserted them in Pamphylia and had not accompanied them in the work. The disagreement became so sharp that they parted company; Barnabas took Mark with him and sailed away to Cyprus. But Paul chose Silas and set out, the believers commending him to the grace of the Lord.

Author Chris Idle once wrote a very funny 'theology of Winnie the Pooh', linking each character to a particular Christian tradition. He decided Rabbit was a Baptist, because he had innumerable small and obscure 'friends and relations'.

We Mennonites are like that too! I'm afraid our tradition has a long history of splits over doctrine or practice, so there are numerous tiny groups bearing the name of whoever led them away from the main group.

This week we are looking at unity between Christian denominations and groupings. The choice to part company with a friend, especially a fellow Christian, can be extremely painful. Even more painful is the choice for a congregation, or a denomination, to divide into two independent groups. We may tell ourselves and others that the split is over a matter of truth or a moral issue, but all too often there are underlying personality clashes,

battles for power or fears of change.

To make up for our history, many Mennonites today are experts in mediation and conflict resolution. The UK Mennonites have a professional service, *Bridgebuilders*, which runs courses in mediation, and goes into churches that are in conflict to lead them through a process of reconciliation. Perhaps if they'd been around in Paul's day…

Thank God, John Mark had the ever-encouraging Barnabas to come alongside him and give him a second chance. God even brought good out of the split, as there were then two mission teams on the road. In most cases, however, God's will is for relationships to be mended and maintained.

Sunday reflection

Where there is hatred, let me sow love; where there is injury, pardon.

Prayer of St Francis

VZ

Us and them

Now I appeal to you, brothers and sisters, by the name of our Lord Jesus Christ, that all of you be in agreement and that there be no divisions among you, but that you be united in the same mind and the same purpose. For it has been reported to me by Chloe's people that there are quarrels among you, my brothers and sisters. What I mean is that each of you says, 'I belong to Paul', or 'I belong to Apollos', or 'I belong to Cephas', or 'I belong to Christ.' Has Christ been divided? Was Paul crucified for you? Or were you baptized in the name of Paul?

I remember my shock when I discovered that there are about 20 Mennonite 'denominations' in the USA and Canada. There are only just over a million Mennonites worldwide—why on earth don't we work together?

Paul must have felt much the same when he realized that even the few thousand Christians in Corinth were already breaking into factions. In fact, he must have felt worse, since this was the first time the Church had experienced division.

When we dream of 'going back to the purity of the early Church', we might do well to remember that our divisions are actually nothing new. Christians have always disagreed over what to believe, how to worship or how to live. Each new group believes itself to be 'the true Church' while the old group probably see themselves as 'the faithful remnant'.

Perhaps organizational unity—a formal reuniting of different churches—will never come. Nevertheless, it is vital to work towards a world where different Christian groupings recognize each other as sincere disciples—or even better, a world where we can all share in communion together as different parts of Christ's body. To see why, we must return to Jesus' great prayer in Gethsemane: 'As you, Father, are in me and I am in you, may they also be in us, *so that the world may believe that you have sent me*' (John 17:21).

Just to encourage you (and myself), it's worth noting that a couple of years ago, the two largest Mennonite groupings formally reunited, after centuries of division. It can be done.

Reflection

Unless we can love each other, no one will believe that God's love is in us.

VZ

Body politics

For just as the body is one and has many members, and all the members of the body, though many, are one body, so it is with Christ. For in the one Spirit we were all baptized into one body— Jews or Greeks, slaves or free—and we were all made to drink of one Spirit. Indeed, the body does not consist of one member but of many. If the foot would say, 'Because I am not a hand, I do not belong to the body', that would not make it any less a part of the body. And if the ear would say, 'Because I am not an eye, I do not belong to the body', that would not make it any less a part of the body. If the whole body were an eye, where would the hearing be? If the whole body were hearing, where would the sense of smell be?

'If the whole body were a foot, how would it smell?' Now we've got that joke out of the way, let's take an offbeat look at this passage. Normally it's applied to relationships within a particular congregation, but how would it be if we applied it, for a change, to relationships between denominations?

I don't think we are entirely departing from Paul's meaning, for at the beginning of this same letter, as we saw yesterday, he was lamenting that the Corinthian church had begun to divide into 'Cephasites and Apollonians'. It's not far from that to Wesleyans, Lutherans and, indeed, Mennonites (named after 17th-century Dutch leader Menno Simons).

So might Paul be saying something like: 'Just because X and Y believe something different about what happens when you share

bread and wine, it doesn't mean they're not Christians or that you have to set up a new group who believe the "right" thing'?

It is not easy to accept that those who believe, worship and live differently from us are actually also part of Jesus' worldwide body; and that if we do not listen to their insights and history, we might be in danger of having only one eye or no teeth. But it just might be what Paul is asking us to do here.

Prayer

Pray for the other denominations represented in your local area and their leaders.

VZ

Not one of us

Then the Gileadites took the fords of the Jordan against the Ephraimites. Whenever one of the fugitives of Ephraim said, 'Let me go over', the men of Gilead would say to him, 'Are you an Ephraimite?' When he said, 'No', they said to him, 'Then say Shibboleth', and he said, 'Sibboleth', for he could not pronounce it right. Then they seized him and killed him at the fords of the Jordan. Forty-two thousand of the Ephraimites fell at that time.

Recently I received an email from someone wanting to join a private Internet bulletin board that I run, for Christians with mental health difficulties: 'I'm wondering if there's some shibboleth thing to this,' he wrote nervously. (I quickly assured him there wasn't.)

The 'password' in this passage has found its way into English to describe any test we impose to determine if someone is, in Mrs Thatcher's celebrated phrase, 'one of us'. ('Is he sound?' used to be the key question asked of any new teacher). Often, we, too, use key words as our litmus test: does she say 'Communion', 'the Lord's table', or 'mass'?

Churches, like any other human groups, are very prone to set up hoops through which prospective members are expected to jump: creeds, bases of faith, doctrinal statements. Then those who don't assent to every jot and tittle can be filtered out. Sometimes this has more to do with our desire to be 'the in group' than with a concern for truth.

Although this Bible story is set in wartime, and so the Gileadites might have had some justification for their action, it's still a brutal story (like many in Judges). I think, too, that it portrays very pithily the tendency we humans have to reject anyone who is 'different'. I still laugh wryly when I remember the statement of a fellow member of the church I attended in Waterloo. It was one of two neighbouring parishes—one traditionally 'low' and one 'high'—served by the same vicar. 'We're Protestant here,' she said. 'They're Anglican up at the other place.'

When we baulk at working with another denomination or condemn them as heretical, let's make sure it's not over a 'shibboleth'.

Prayer

Father of all, help me to accept those who don't think or act the way I do.

VZ

The ins and outs

Now concerning spiritual gifts, brothers and sisters, I do not want you to be uninformed. You know that when you were pagans, you were enticed and led astray to idols that could not speak. Therefore I want you to understand that no one speaking by the Spirit of God ever says 'Let Jesus be cursed!' and no one can say 'Jesus is Lord' except by the Holy Spirit. Now there are varieties of gifts, but the same Spirit; and there are varieties of services, but the same Lord; and there are varieties of activities, but it is the same God who activates all of them in everyone. To each is given the manifestation of the Spirit for the common good.

I know several people who have refused to be speakers for a particular organization, because they felt they could not in conscience sign its basis of faith, required of all speakers. Some just didn't agree with all of it; some felt it was over-controlling to 'vet' people in this way, and some thought that if the Nicene or the Apostles' Creed was good enough for most churches, it ought to be good enough for a parachurch organization. I have a lot of sympathy with them.

Of course, it's important for a church to formulate its core convictions and to expect members to share them. The trouble comes when we dismiss any other group whose convictions vary slightly from ours. In contrast, Paul's criterion for who is 'sound' seem remarkably simple and inclusive. If someone says 'Jesus be cursed', they're not a Christian or a Christian group; if they say 'Jesus is Lord', they are. To put it another way: if it walks like a duck and quacks like a duck… it's a duck.

What? No statement on the nature of the Trinity? No explanation of the atonement? No mention of the second coming? Just 'Jesus is Lord'?

All right, I know this is about recognizing spiritual gifts, not about denominations. Here's a thought: might we recognize the validity of other denominations by the spiritual gifts they display? Or even just by the fact that they, like us, say 'Jesus is Lord'?

Reflection

'Now the Lord is the Spirit, and where the Spirit of the Lord is, there is freedom' (2 Corinthians 3:17).

VZ

MATTHEW 7:15–21 (NRSV)

Look for the fruit

[Jesus said] 'Beware of false prophets, who come to you in sheep's clothing but inwardly are ravenous wolves. You will know them by their fruits. Are grapes gathered from thorns, or figs from thistles? In the same way, every good tree bears good fruit, but the bad tree bears bad fruit. A good tree cannot bear bad fruit, nor can a bad tree bear good fruit. Every tree that does not bear good fruit is cut down and thrown into the fire. Thus you will know them by their fruits. Not everyone who says to me, "Lord, Lord", will enter the kingdom of heaven, but only the one who does the will of my Father in heaven.'

Many years ago my husband was excommunicated. It didn't worry him too much, as it was from a group (the Christadelphians) from which he had already begun to distance himself. One of the things that got him into trouble was preaching on 'Welcome one another… just as Christ has welcomed you' (Romans 15:7) and suggesting that his hearers should accept other denominations as Christian.

You may ask, isn't it important to make alliances only with those who are on the same path as us? Might not some who claim to be Christians actually be misled and mislead others? There are indeed groups who teach strange and doubtful things. There are also some whose doctrine is totally orthodox, yet who are soaked through with legalism and pride.

Jesus here seems remarkably unconcerned about what people believe. He's much more interested in whether or not they are living the Jesus lifestyle of love, simplicity and self-sacrifice. If they are, it is safe to work with them.

I don't think he said this so that we could exercise our right to condemn those whom we don't think are fruitful! I think he said it so that we could recognize where he is at work and join in. Where there is good fruit—care for the poor, forgiveness, lives made new—that's where he is—not necessarily where they have impeccable teaching, or even impressive healings. Doctrine isn't everything, thank God.

Today is Women's World Day of Prayer, on the theme 'United under God's tent'. Somehow, I feel Jesus wouldn't exclude anyone from praying together.

Prayer

Lord, may my actions, not just my words, show that I'm a Jesus person.

VZ

One at last

And I heard the number of those who were sealed, one hundred forty-four thousand, sealed out of every tribe of the people of Israel… After this I looked, and there was a great multitude that no one could count, from every nation, from all tribes and peoples and languages, standing before the throne and before the Lamb, robed in white, with palm branches in their hands. They cried out in a loud voice, saying, 'Salvation belongs to our God who is seated on the throne, and to the Lamb!'

Something has puzzled me for a long time. First of all, why do those who claim that only 144,000 will be saved not notice that all those 144,000 are Jewish? (So I'm in, but most of them aren't…!) Second, how could they fail to spot, just a few verses later, the mention of the 'great multitude that no one could count'?

There is an old joke about someone being shown round heaven and seeing the lovely spots where each of the denominations have set up their camp. Finally, they are shown a high wall, behind which a particular denomination (which I won't name for fear of repercussions), are clustered, singing hymns. 'That's the X', says the guide. 'Don't talk too loudly, they think they're the only ones here.' You've probably heard it with a number of different groups identified as 'X'!

I will let you into a secret: there are no Methodists in heaven. Nor Catholics, Baptists nor even Mennonites (although we, of course, have the best chance—that's a joke, in case you missed it). There are only Christians. In the 'great multitude' who fall on their faces before the Lamb and shout out their praises to God, all denominational barriers, all disagreements about what this or that verse means or about the correct way to swing a censer or if a censer is a tool of the devil, disappear in a huge wave of love for the one who has lived, died and risen for us.

Nice thought, isn't it? Though 'nice' is perhaps an inadequate word…

Prayer

'The glory that you have given me I have given them, so that they may be one, as we are one, I in them and you in me, that they may become completely one' (John 17:22–23).
Father, answer Jesus' prayer through us. Amen

VZ

Don't forget to renew your annual subscription to *New Daylight*! If you enjoy the notes, why not also consider giving a gift subscription to a friend or member of your family?

See page 153 for details of a FREE BOOK offer with each gift subscription.

You will find a subscription order form overleaf.
New Daylight is also available from your local Christian bookshop.

❑ I would like to take out a subscription myself (complete your name and address details only once)

❑ I would like to give a gift subscription (please complete both name and address sections below), with a FREE copy of *Long Wandering Prayer*.

Your name _____

Your address_____

_____Postcode_____

Gift subscription name _____

Gift subscription address_____

_____Postcode_____

Please send *New Daylight* beginning with the May / September 2007 / January 2008 issue: (delete as applicable)

(please tick box)	UK	SURFACE	AIR MAIL
NEW DAYLIGHT	❑ £12.75	❑ £14.10	❑ £16.35
NEW DAYLIGHT 3-year sub	❑ £30.00		
NEW DAYLIGHT DELUXE	❑ £17.10	❑ £20.70	❑ £25.20

I would like to take out an annual subscription to *Quiet Spaces* beginning with the next available issue:

(please tick box)	UK	SURFACE	AIR MAIL
QUIET SPACES	❑ £16.95	❑ £18.45	❑ £20.85

Please complete the payment details below and send your coupon, with appropriate payment, to: **BRF, First Floor, Elsfield Hall, 15–17 Elsfield Way, Oxford OX2 8FG.**

Total enclosed £ _____ (cheques should be made payable to 'BRF')

Payment by cheque ❑ postal order ❑ Visa ❑ Mastercard ❑ Switch ❑

Card number: ☐☐☐☐☐☐☐☐☐☐☐☐☐☐☐☐☐☐

Expiry date of card: ☐☐☐☐   Issue number (Switch): ☐☐☐☐

Signature (essential if paying by credit/Switch card)_____

❑ Please do not send me further information about BRF publications.

BRF resources are available from your local Christian bookshop. BRF is a Registered Charity

2 Corinthians 8—10

For the next fortnight we shall be considering 2 Corinthians 8—10, and we have the opportunity to read the whole text—it has not been necessary to leave anything out of these three chapters for reasons of space! In the first part of 2 Corinthians Paul describes his spiritual labours and other activities, and we can identify a genuine affection for the Corinthian church. In chapters 8—9 he broaches the thorny subject of stewardship—the giving of money to support the Judean Christians. Then, from chapter 10 on, Paul evidently felt the need to defend his spiritual credentials, and even to attack the Corinthians, which he does at the close of the book (chapter 13).

There has been much discussion and some controversy about how 2 Corinthians came to be. Some people argue that, like 1 Corinthians and Romans, it is a complete and singular letter, written by Paul around AD55. While Paul's authorship is rarely disputed, there are scholars who claim that 2 Corinthians is not a single letter, being constructed of two or more letters, which may not have been written at the same time. In 2 Corinthians 2:3–4 Paul mentions a 'sorrowful letter', which he felt the need to write to the church. This letter is not now thought by many to be 1 Corinthians, and we have to take into account the possibility that letters from Paul have been lost to history. It may be the case that the letter Paul refers to was not lost after all, but was later incorporated into what we now have in our Bibles as 2 Corinthians. If so, chapters 10—13 are a prime suspect in this case, mainly because of a change in style of writing and discrepancies in the way in which Paul refers to events and to himself. In the first nine chapters he is quite modest, giving the impression that he does not need to commend himself to his audience, because he has already done so (see 3:1 and 5:12). Yet in 10—13, he is less reticent about his credentials and is even quite bold, sounding critical of the Corinthians' narrow-minded and self-indulgent ways.

Thus we encounter two different, but related sides of Paul's character, through which we can discover valuable insights into the nature of Christian financial stewardship and mission, many of which seem as relevant to us as they were to him.

Gordon Giles

Joining together

We want you to know, brothers and sisters, about the grace of God that has been granted to the churches of Macedonia; for during a severe ordeal of affliction, their abundant joy and their extreme poverty have overflowed in a wealth of generosity on their part. For, as I can testify, they voluntarily gave according to their means, and even beyond their means, begging us earnestly for the privilege of sharing in this ministry to the saints—and this, not merely as we expected; they gave themselves first to the Lord and, by the will of God, to us, so that we might urge Titus that, as he had already made a beginning, so he should also complete this generous undertaking among you.

This letter cannot have been easy for Paul to write. 1 Corinthians reveals that he was dealing with an adventurous, even unruly bunch who, having converted to Christianity, needed support, encouragement and sometimes reprimand. Paul has to assert the truth of the gospel and defend his own credentials in both instructing and telling them off. The beginning of chapter 8 opens a key section of the letter, in which Paul introduces a very practical task in hand: the financial support of poor and afflicted churches in Judea. The Corinthians are, of course, Gentiles, like the Macedonians who have already expressed a willingness to give and whose example Paul is promoting.

Such charity still exists today: our parish supports a project in Mozambique called *Imagine*. Founded after the terrible floods of 2000, it provides resources for schooling and housing. Personal contacts exist between the two congregations in London and Maputo, indicating a deep commitment and friendship between the two communities. This is by no means unique: other churches do likewise.

Thus, as well as revealing generosity and Christian charity on the surface, Paul is promoting unity through charitable connectedness. By joining together in a charitable effort, those who do so are united not only in spiritual faith, but in common practical purpose. When one church gives to another, bonds of fellowship and care are created, uniting giver and receiver in faith and action.

Sunday reflection

Lord, let us give together, that we may share together, in faith and works. Amen

GG

Double appeal

Now as you excel in everything—in faith, in speech, in knowledge, in utmost eagerness, and in our love for you—so we want you to excel also in this generous undertaking. I do not say this as a command, but I am testing the genuineness of your love against the earnestness of others. For you know the generous act of our Lord Jesus Christ, that though he was rich, yet for your sakes he became poor, so that by his poverty you might become rich. And in this matter I am giving my advice: it is appropriate for you who began last year not only to do something but even to desire to do something— now finish doing it, so that your eagerness may be matched by completing it according to your means.

Flattery will get you anywhere or so the saying goes! Paul is a bit cleverer than that, though, for he appeals not only to the Corinthians' abilities and gifts, but also to their better nature. He appeals primarily to their love, for himself and, more surreptitiously, for themselves. For Paul is asking them to match the generosity of the Macedonians, thereby gaining some kudos. He threatens their reputation (for the Corinthians had pledged their support) and is now calling in that pledge. Polite and kind as he is, Paul needs them to honour their offer because he has promised to deliver their charity. He has taken the risk of playing the Macedonians and Corinthians off against one another, thereby inspiring each to a spirit of love and generosity.

Paul's approach is still used today. Have you ever been phoned in a telethon? Polite and pleasant people offer praise and persuade us to part with a pledge. Then, later, cajoling reminders encourage us to follow up what we agreed. A similar technique is used on the major television fundraising shows. Notice that we call them 'appeals'—a double-edged word. Our generosity is appealed to, but in an attractive or amusing way that 'appeals' to us. Witness the success of Comic Relief!

While Paul is no comedian, like his modern successors, he knows how to appeal in a loving, effective way.

Prayer

Lord, give us grace that we may be made generous by the appeals of your children in need. Amen

GG

Money talks

For if the eagerness is there, the gift is acceptable according to what one has—not according to what one does not have. I do not mean that there should be relief for others and pressure on you, but it is a question of a fair balance between your present abundance and their need, so that their abundance may be for your need, in order that there may be a fair balance. As it is written, 'The one who had much did not have too much, and the one who had little did not have too little.' But thanks be to God who put in the heart of Titus the same eagerness for you that I myself have.

When I was little I remember being told that there are two things one shouldn't ask someone: how old they are and how much they earn! Paul, however, is happy to talk money with the young church of Corinth. He wants to ensure that they do not think what they give will be squandered or that they will become poor while others grow rich. Yet, as we read yesterday, this is what Christ did spiritually—made himself poor so that others might become rich (8:9). Paul doesn't want anyone to be made physically rich or poor, which is why he prefers to seek a bit of gentle redistribution of wealth that he knows will make all the difference to the Judean Christians without embarrassing or causing hardship elsewhere.

Wealth is and always has been a relative issue. In his influential and satirical novel, *The Bonfire of the Vanities*, Tom Wolfe describes how one might find it hard to get by on a mere million dollars per annum! Meanwhile half the world's population have to manage on less than three dollars a day. In Paul's day the discrepancy was perhaps not so great, but one community could still help another. Today the gap between rich and poor is very great and, if Paul can tell the Corinthians of his day that there is no excuse for not giving, how much more apposite is his advice for us?

Circumstances may determine our material wealth, but we are spiritually richer if we share what we have.

Prayer

*Lord, all that we have comes from you, and of your own, we share.
Amen*

GG

Poor impressions

For [Titus] not only accepted our appeal, but since he is more eager than ever, he is going to you of his own accord. With him we are sending the brother who is famous among all the churches for his proclaiming of the good news; and not only that, but he has also been appointed by the churches to travel with us while we are administering this generous undertaking for the glory of the Lord himself and to show our goodwill. We intend that no one should blame us about this generous gift that we are administering, for we intend to do what is right not only in the Lord's sight but also in the sight of others.

There is no doubt that Paul was a shrewd operator, well-versed in the ways of the world as well as the way of the Lord. He did not learn it all on the Damascus road either: before being blinded by the light of Christ (Acts 9) he had been clever and cunning in his commitment to the suppression of emergent Christianity. Thus there is no reason to suppose that Paul had a personality transplant when he turned to Christ. Far from it—it was precisely because of his characteristic gifts that he was called by God to take the gospel to the Gentiles, founding and fostering new churches.

Here Paul is open about what he is doing—he is sending someone who he knows will be respected, because he knows that the impression given can make or break his mission. Paul needs to impress other people in order to further this practical Christian objective of helping the poor. He also knows that he must not only do the right thing and help them, but must be seen to do so.

While it may be true that God knows the quiet generosity of the heart, it can be harmful to the reputation of the gospel if churches and their leaders are thought to be mean or uncaring, because everything is done in secret. It seems to have been the case for Paul at this point in his ministry: he needed everyone to know and understand how and why the new churches were to help each other.

Prayer

Let our generosity be genuine Lord, for the good of your gospel. Amen

GG

Love and money

And with them we are sending our brother whom we have often tested and found eager in many matters, but who is now more eager than ever because of his great confidence in you. As for Titus, he is my partner and co-worker in your service; as for our brothers, they are messengers of the churches, the glory of Christ. Therefore, openly before the churches, show them the proof of your love and of our reason for boasting about you.

A few years ago a group of Cambridge University students decided to sell the friendship of one of their contemporaries on the eBay Internet site. 'Big John' as they called him, unwittingly had his friendship auctioned online and amassed for them the princely sum of £22. For this, the successful bidder acquired a 'Big John friendship pack', which included a badge declaring that 'I'm Big John's friend' and a specially recorded tape of his most famous catchphrases, such as 'You coming down the pub later?' Perhaps fittingly, the friendship pack included a £3 voucher entitling the buyer to one drink with Big John.

Money isn't everything. Love, as Paul has already told the people of Corinth (1 Corinthians 13), counts for far more. You can't buy or sell love—it must be genuine. As such it is priceless and it endures. These days we tend to treat friendship as a lesser emotion than love, with the view that love evolves from friendship, and this makes Paul's words seem odd. This is unfortunate, because friendship *is* love and should be equally valued.

Here in the name and spirit of love and friendship, Paul sends Titus and others, and we can imagine that Paul has sent them with similar sentiments to those with which he hopes they will be received. He has certainly 'boasted' to them that they can expect to be warmly received. Even though they are beloved ambassadors, they also have a real and important task—to secure funding without undermining the real bonds of fellowship and friendship that exist between them and Paul and between Paul and the Corinthian church. For if the bonds of love are strong, then the money is sure to follow.

Prayer

Lord, fund us with your love, that we may be generous in heart and mind.
Amen

GG

A round tuit

Now it is not necessary for me to write to you about the ministry to the saints, for I know your eagerness, which is the subject of my boasting about you to the people of Macedonia, saying that Achaia has been ready since last year; and your zeal has stirred up most of them. But I am sending the brothers in order that our boasting about you may not prove to have been empty in this case, so that you may be ready, as I said you would be; otherwise, if some Macedonians come with me and find that you are not ready, we would be humiliated—to say nothing of you—in this undertaking.

Have you ever promised to help someone but never got around to it? Have others let you down in this way? In some shops they sell a piece of pottery, either a mug or paperweight, called 'a round tuit'. Perhaps somebody has bought you one—just so that you can say 'I've got a round tuit'!

Well, Paul certainly has got a round tuit—and although he says it is not necessary for him to remind them, it is clearly necessary to get them a round tuit too! Paul is using one of those expressions still very familiar today: 'of course, it goes without saying that…'. We use these kinds of expressions to disguise the fact that we do think it needs saying. We soften the blow, as it were, because, embarrassing as it is, we sometimes need to remind people of a favour or promise they haven't yet fulfilled. Sometimes there are things that we have undertaken but not yet carried out and that we need reminding about. It's like that for Paul, who sends emissaries to encourage the Corinthians to cough up, because if they don't, they will all be embarrassed.

Can you think of a similar situation as far as you are concerned? Have you promised a donation to a charity or offered or been asked to do something that you have not yet done? Are you putting it off, or is it that you simply haven't got a round tuit? Do go out and get one…

Prayer

Lord, we thank you for the generosity and service of friends. May we be faithful in our fellowship and generous with our love. Amen

GG

Cheerful giving

So I thought it necessary to urge the brothers to go on ahead to you, and arrange in advance for this bountiful gift that you have promised, so that it may be ready as a voluntary gift and not as an extortion. The point is this: the one who sows sparingly will also reap sparingly, and the one who sows bountifully will also reap bountifully. Each of you must give as you have made up your mind, not reluctantly or under compulsion, for God loves a cheerful giver. And God is able to provide you with every blessing in abundance, so that by always having enough of everything, you may share abundantly in every good work.

Perhaps like me you have had someone say 'God loves a cheerful giver' to you as an attempt to exploit your generosity. As a vicar, I have people knocking on my door from time to time, asking for money or help, and it can be hard to know what is best. If wearing a dog collar in London, I am a soft target, but it is not practical, safe or possible to hand out cash, even if the apostle Paul himself is invoked!

Street begging is a painful issue. Apparent destitution, real need and pastoral difficulties are often involved, but there are often niggling doubts that some kind of scam is being pulled. Many therefore refrain from giving in the street, preferring to donate to organized charities instead, and this they do cheerfully. There is another difficulty, however—for some say that organized charities take too much in administration charges, while there clearly are people suffering on the streets.

What is interesting, if you read this passage carefully, is that Paul doesn't care about these arguments and he offers no specific advice. Some people run a charity account with the Charities Aid Foundation (CAF), which means they can cheerfully write out cheques drawing on money already allocated for the purpose. Others hand out cash readily, and perhaps many of us do a mixture of both.

Whatever we do, two things are important—to give something, and to rid ourselves of angst as and when we do so. Relax and be generous, for God loves everyone, giver and receiver alike.

Prayer

Freely as we have received, may we freely give love. Amen

GG

2 CORINTHIANS 9:9–12 (NRSV)

Harvest help

As it is written, 'He scatters abroad, he gives to the poor; his right-eousness endures forever.' He who supplies seed to the sower and bread for food will supply and multiply your seed for sowing and increase the harvest of your righteousness. You will be enriched in every way for your great generosity, which will produce thanksgiving to God through us; for the rendering of this ministry not only sup-plies the needs of the saints but also overflows with many thanks-givings to God.

Biblical references to harvest are plentiful, the most famous being Jesus' parable of the sower (Luke 8:5–15). Paul follows a good prece-dent, but more importantly, he is speaking a familiar language. Like so many civilizations before and since, Asia Minor relied on agricul-ture, and most of the employment was found in the fields. The harvest was brief and intense, so most labour was casual.

The normal day's wage for a working man was about 4p. Even allowing for various differences in prices and costs of living, 4p a day was not a wage that left much room for financial manoeuvre. If there was no work, there was no money, and to be unemployed for a day was disastrous. There are still many places today for which this remains true, where countries tend to have subsistence, agricultural economies, where the exigencies of harvest are paramount.

Bearing this in mind, Paul seeks funding for poor Christians in Judea. Whether they labour in the Lord's vineyard, or in the real fields, they have little and need help. If the Corinthians give from their bounty, it is not only an act of generosity, but also an act of gratitude for their fellowship and faith. Furthermore, if they give, God's generosity is manifest in them. Their generosity is God's generosity.

So it is for us. As Teresa of Avila once wrote: 'Christ has no body now on earth but yours, no hands but yours, no feet but yours; yours are the eyes through which Christ's compassion looks out on the world, yours are the feet with which he is to go about doing good and yours are the hands with which he is to bless us now.' This is as true now as it ever was.

Sunday reflection

Let us use our hands, feet, eyes, hearts and money to God's glory.

GG

Ineffable expressibility

Through the testing of this ministry you glorify God by your obedience to the confession of the gospel of Christ and by the generosity of your sharing with them and with all others, while they long for you and pray for you because of the surpassing grace of God that he has given you. Thanks be to God for his indescribable gift!

Actions speak louder than words. Having hinted this, Paul now attributes the same idea to God, whose action in Christ, and in enabling their generosity, is 'inexpressible'. Remarkably, the word Paul uses (*anekdiegetos*) was not known to his contemporaries nor the ancient Greeks. This verse is the first and only place where it appears. In order to express the inexpressibility of God's abundance, he invents a new word! His enthusiasm is infectious and we can sense his excitement as he concludes this part of his correspondence on a confident, grateful note. As a later reference in Romans reveals, his confidence and excitement are well-founded, for he has presented a very persuasive case to inspire his audience's generosity (Romans 15:25–26). Through that success, God is glorified and Paul is gratified.

This is no ancient emotion that we see in Paul: we can all feel like this. It is delightful to persuade someone to take a different view, wonderful to share in their discovery of faith. Yet, when we are committed to something, there are often times when what seems so obvious and right is dismissed by others. On another level, some do not share our enthusiasms for sports teams, artworks, pieces of music or parts of the world. When enabled to share our enthusiasms and, even better, to encounter others who respond to them, it can be a truly uplifting and affirming experience as like minds 'click'.

Paul is on a high, so he offers praise and glory to God on high. This is natural and easy. But, as we shall see, things are about to change for Paul in the next chapter, and he must take a different tone. For now, though, let us rejoice with him that the rich shall help the poor in a spirit of Christian love and fellowship, giving Paul the credit and God the glory!

Prayer

What we cannot say, Lord, enable us to do, that all may offer you praise. Amen

GG

Tuesday 13 March

2 CORINTHIANS 10:1–4 (NRSV)

On message

I myself, Paul, appeal to you by the meekness and gentleness of Christ—I who am humble when face to face with you, but bold towards you when I am away!—I ask that when I am present I need not show boldness by daring to oppose those who think we are acting according to human standards. Indeed, we live as human beings, but we do not wage war according to human standards; for the weapons of our warfare are not merely human, but they have divine power to destroy strongholds.

Paul has changed his tone now, moving from praise and thanksgiving to God and the Corinthians to a sterner approach. Textual scholars have suggested that with chapter 10 begins a separate, harsher letter, written before or after chapters 1—9. Here we see Paul reintroducing himself, appealing personally, as if to say, 'Look, friends, it is I, Paul, whom you know of old'. It is clear that there has been some trouble in the past, of which there has been no hint in the previous chapter.

The suggestion, which Paul seems to quote, is that he is distantly severe with them, but humble in their presence. In our technological age we have the same problem—emails can be sent so swiftly that we can fire a message off without giving enough consideration to how it will be read. Communication, it is said, is not about what the speaker says, but what the receiver hears. Where fast, written communication occurs it can be so easy to misjudge things

and emails can amplify this risk. Sometimes when we meet someone we have emailed a few times, we can be surprised at what they are like—they may turn out to be far nicer (or less so!) than their online manner would have us believe.

Paul acknowledges the apparent difference between his near and distant presence, but wants to remind his audience that, while this may be an inevitable consequence of human forms of communication, he and they are accountable to a higher authority, and divine truth is far more important than trivial debates about personality traits. Ultimately it is not the medium they should worry about, but the message—the message of redemption through Jesus Christ.

Prayer

Jesus, you are the medium and the message of our salvation. Hear us and guide us. Amen

GG

Personal issues

We destroy arguments and every proud obstacle raised up against the knowledge of God, and we take every thought captive to obey Christ. We are ready to punish every disobedience when your obedience is complete. Look at what is before your eyes. If you are confident that you belong to Christ, remind yourself of this, that just as you belong to Christ, so also do we.

Paul's manners or modes of communication are all devoted to the service of Christ and, as far as he is concerned, this is all that matters. While his readers may be convinced of their own status, the fact that some of them do not like his methods does not entitle them to dismiss his Christian witness, teaching or maturity.

Paul's predicament is still with us today. It is soul-destroying to read of factions in the church community, with some individuals or groups declaring others to be beyond the pale theologically, biblically, morally or spiritually. There is and must be a place for discussion of lifestyle, doctrinal and ethical issues and Christians are confronted by so many matters that cut to the heart of attitudes concerning the beginning and end of life, relationships and global welfare.

Different perspectives can become polarized into mini-communities, however, with each wedded to a particular position, so that criticism of or engagement with that point of view can easily be seen as a criticism of the community itself. Arguments become personal, jeopardizing both relationship and rationality. Under these circumstances, trust and empathy are eroded, and the chance of progress towards a common goal or understanding is minimized. Perhaps, like Paul's detractors, we have lost the ability to discuss issues properly, being tempted instead to focus on the personalities involved. Today's cult of celebrity exemplifies this. While pastoral issues are important, so are moral and theological thought and practice, which cannot and should not be sidelined.

Paul reminds his detractors that just as they are Christians, so is he. This lies at the root of all that transpires between them, just as it does for Christians and churches today.

Prayer

Lord, comfort and lead your Christian community in mutual love and gospel truth. Amen

GG

Barking and biting

Now, even if I boast a little too much of our authority, which the Lord gave for building you up and not for tearing you down, I will not be ashamed of it. I do not want to seem as though I am trying to frighten you with my letters. For they say, 'His letters are weighty and strong, but his bodily presence is weak, and his speech contemptible.' Let such people understand that what we say by letter when absent, we will also do when present.

Paul has gained a reputation—his bark is worse than his bite. Those who did not like his approach and wanted to undermine his authority were saying that there was a serious discrepancy between the way he dealt with them in person and by letter: 'This is not the Paul we know,' they say.

So what was Paul really like? The second-century apocryphal text, the Acts of Paul and Thecla, describes Paul as a thin-haired, short man, with crooked legs, joined eyebrows and a slightly hooked nose. He does not seem to have had a frightening appearance. Yet they had probably not encountered him when, as Saul of Tarsus, he inspired fear among Christians (see Acts 8:3; 9:1–2, 13, 26). Although Paul was a passionate man, those against him did not credit him for it, preferring the apparently mild-mannered guest that visited them. This apparent discrepancy in Paul's behaviour was used to discredit him. Even though he writes strongly in this passage (and elsewhere!), some of his readers concluded that the written Paul is not the real Paul, and so can be ignored.

We can imagine how frustrating this must have been. Paul threatens them with the same severity that they do not believe possible, attempting to assure them that if necessary he can and will be harsh. If so, they will have brought it upon themselves, like errant children who call their parents' bluff and then regret it! Paul is their father in God, as it were, and it must have pained him to be severe at times, but for him their spiritual protection and development were the main priority, rather than simply being considered a 'nice bloke'.

Prayer

God, you are both near us and far from us. Build us up in love and hope. Amen

GG

Inhuman competition

We do not dare to classify or compare ourselves with some of those who commend themselves. But when they measure themselves by one another, and compare themselves with one another, they do not show good sense. We, however, will not boast beyond limits, but will keep within the field that God has assigned to us, to reach out even as far as you. For we were not overstepping our limits when we reached you; we were the first to come all the way to you with the good news of Christ.

The Corinthians were judging one another like spiritual athletes in a human arena. Before Corinth was destroyed by Roman troops in 146BC, it had been a centre of commerce and sport, hosting the biennial Isthmian Games. When Julius Caesar rebuilt the city a century later, the games returned to the Roman capital of the Greek region of Achaia—Corinth was a competitive place.

Paul refused to play their game. He argued that the limits of human behaviour and spirituality are set by God; they are not targets to overleap or benchmarks to beat. Fellow Christians are co-workers, perhaps under obedience or tuition, but they are not rivals. If they become so, there is a good chance that issues will give way to personality conflicts. This is what happened in Corinth from time to time, causing Paul distress and difficulty.

Today we have this problem in two forms. We have seen how debates can get personal, losing focus on what is really at stake. Sometimes, however, the opposite happens—a rigorous investigation into the rights and wrongs of an issue can so ignore the feelings and perspectives of the people involved that it becomes inhuman. It is common now to distinguish between the sin and the sinner, placing the sinner (the person) to one side while judging the sin. This approach has a flaw, which is that the humanity of the person, a sinner like you or me, is dismantled in the process. Our weaknesses contribute to our identity and if we ignore or separate them, we are relating to others in a dishonest, fragmented way. In a balanced society we should be wary of both extremes.

Prayer

Lord, as your faithful team on earth, may we be united in purpose and praise. Amen

GG

2 Corinthians 10:15–18 (NRSV)

Boasters

We do not boast beyond limits, that is, in the labours of others; but our hope is that, as your faith increases, our sphere of action among you may be greatly enlarged, so that we may proclaim the good news in lands beyond you, without boasting of work already done in someone else's sphere of action. 'Let the one who boasts, boast in the Lord.' For it is not those who commend themselves that are approved, but those whom the Lord commends.

Do you like those biscuits known as Boasters? A zany website describes them as the best in the world, after a 'world cup of biscuit tasting' in which they beat off Golden Crunch Creams in the final. Not surprisingly I suppose, they are 'boasters' after all! As we saw yesterday the spirit of competition was at large in Corinth, and competitive people often brag about their successes. Worse still, they sometimes boast about others' triumphs, even claiming them as their own. This seems to be what was happening in Christian Corinth. A certain pride was being taken: 'I've set up more churches than he has'; 'I've brought a dozen families into the church'.

Paul is not so petty, nor so unambitious. There is a wide world out there, where no one is working, so he is annoyed that they are competing on such a small turf! Soon after, when writing from Corinth to the Romans, he indicated his intention to visit Spain to spread the gospel (Romans 15:24). Spain was certainly a 'land beyond you'.

The bigger picture gives perspective to the little ecclesiastical 'successes' of which some of the Corinthians were so proud. It is an honour and a delight to nurture someone new in the faith, but the experience should not be exaggerated. There are so many to whom the gospel has not been taken and the failure of the Church to reach them, in the first or 21st century, is hardly something to boast about. Some churches today expect their members to bring a steady flow of converts into the Christian community, even promoting a sort of competition. Yet, in our current quasi-pagan climate, we need the guidance of the Spirit. Any reward is in the Lord, not in self-congratulation. Therefore boasting really does take the biscuit!

Prayer
Into your hands, O Lord, we commend our service. Amen

GG

Judges 17—21

The book of Judges tells the story of Israel immediately after the time of Joshua and the entry into the promised land and before the establishment of the monarchy. Tradition has it that it was written by Samuel the prophet. It should have been a happy tale of progress and triumph; instead it is a shameful narrative of darkness and defeat.

Choosing not to rid the land of the depraved Canaanite tribes, the Israelites settled instead for peaceful co-existence and it ruined them. Forsaking their own distinctive expression of faith, they were drawn into the religious ways of their neighbours, with devastating consequences. What we call the 'Judges cycle' was set in motion.

This cycle consisted of disobedience to God in the form of syncretistic worship (mixing Canaanite ways with their own), which in turn led to defeat in battle by one or other of the neighbouring tribes. Humiliated, the Israelites called out to God in their distress and asked for his help. In his mercy he rescued them, raising up a deliverer (or judge) to set them free and restore them to a proper faith in God. Unfortunately, after a period of faithfulness, they tended to slip back into their old ways and the cycle began all over again.

Thus we have the stories of Othniel, Ehud, Deborah, Gideon, Jephthah and Samson; and the oft-repeated episodes of disobedience, defeat, distress and deliverance.

The section we are studying (chapters 17—21) comes at the very end of the book and is often described as an epilogue or appendix. These chapters describe some very dark days indeed when no deliverer appears on the scene to guide the nation back to the ways of God. Instead the chaos and confusion create within the writer the longing for a king, someone to provide stability and order and a renewal of faith (see 17:6; 18:1; 19:1 and 21:25).

It is not particularly easy to draw spiritual inspiration from such a depressing period of Israelite history. Perhaps the one big lesson is that disobedience to God will always have negative consequences, while submission to his rule provides us with the wisest and safest way to live. This applies to individuals, as well as to whole societies.

Isn't it better to learn from the mistakes of others than to repeat those same mistakes and learn from bitter experience?

Tony Horsfall

No king in Israel

In those days Israel had no king; everyone did as he saw fit.

Has Samuel changed his mind as he writes this history? The prophet is often regarded as having been opposed to the monarchy, interpreting the enthronement of Saul as a rejection of God as king, but this is not necessarily the case. What Samuel objected to was the motive behind Israel's request for a king (simply to be like the other nations), and his warning was of the dangers that would befall the nation if the king were not God's choice.

In fact the book of Deuteronomy makes it clear that the right person as king would be a means of blessing to Israel. It would need to be someone chosen by God who would rule on the basis of God's law and with humility and reverence (see Deuteronomy 17:14–20). What is in mind for Israel is not so much a monarchy (where an individual rules), but a theocracy (where the king rules under God). The crisis in Israel is seen as proof that the nation needs a godly leader to bring them together again and provide a clear spiritual direction.

Perhaps the moral chaos of our own postmodern times can be diagnosed in a similar fashion to this period in Israel's history. The rejection of objective moral standards, such as the ten commandments, means effectively that people nowadays do whatever they themselves deem to be right. Morality has become a matter of personal opinion, and anything goes.

This verse reminds us of the importance of good government. It is why we are told to pray for kings and all who are in authority, that we may live in the kind of peace and security that promotes holy living (1 Timothy 2:1–2). It is why we are to be good citizens, supporting the rule of law (Romans 13:1–7).

It also reminds us of the importance of leadership at all levels of society and especially in the Church. Leadership is never an easy task. It is often a lonely business, and it is easier to criticize from the sidelines than to lead from the front. Those who are called to lead, whether locally or nationally, deserve our prayers and our support.

Sunday prayer

Lord, grant wisdom to all who are in positions of leadership, both in your Church and in our society. Amen

TH

A prodigal son

Now a man named Micah from the hill country of Ephraim said to his mother, 'The eleven hundred shekels of silver that were taken from you and about which I heard you utter a curse—I have the silver with me; I took it.' Then his mother said, 'The Lord bless you, my son!'... Now this man Micah had a shrine, and he made an ephod and some idols and installed one of his sons as his priest.

We are given an illustration first of the moral chaos that existed in Israel at an individual level and in family life.

A man admits to stealing from his own mother a huge amount of money, presumably her life savings. Then, having received her forgiveness and with her agreement, he makes an idol with some of the silver for his homemade shrine.

It is clear that for Micah, his god is money. The sin of avarice has gripped his heart to such an extent that he deliberately chooses to dishonour his mother and to steal from her. We know that money itself is not wrong; it is the love of money that is a root of all kinds of evil (1 Timothy 6:10). That love has possessed Micah's soul, and its poisonous root is already bearing fruit in his life. Presently, he will learn from bitter experience some of the griefs that pierce the souls of those who tread the path of greed (see the reading for 22 March).

Ironically, money is his god in a literal way with the fashioning of the silver idol, which he adds to his collection. He sets up his own personal shrine, with his son as priest, complete with ephod (a priestly garment). Religion is important to him, but he wants a god he can control and, we learn later, a god who will be good to him (see 17:13). Where now the pure thought of worshipping the one true God alone? Where now the rejection of graven images?

Money and religion do not mix well, yet there have always been those who want to marry the two, usually for personal gain. The saying remains true, however 'you cannot serve both God and Money' (Matthew 6:24).

Prayer

Lord, keep my heart free from the love of money and from manipulating you for my own ends.
Amen

TH

A prodigal priest

A young Levite from Bethlehem in Judah, who had been living within the clan of Judah, left that town in search of some other place to stay. On his way he came to Micah's house in the hill country of Ephraim… Then Micah said to him, 'Live with me and be my father and priest, and I'll give you ten shekels of silver a year, your clothes and your food.' So the Levite agreed to live with him.

What motivates people in ministry?

It should be the desire to glorify God and serve other people. Sadly, this is not always the case, and this second story about Micah, this time concerning a young Levite from Bethlehem, illustrates the religious corruption in Israel, and the danger of mixed motives.

The tribe of Levi had been set apart to serve God. As such they received no land inheritance, but were supported by the gifts and tithes of the people. They were free to move around and teach the ways of God wherever he led them to settle (see Deuteronomy 18:6–8).

The Levite in this story is later identified as a direct descendant of Moses, called Jonathan son of Gershom (18:30). We are not told what caused him to move from Bethlehem, but we are given the impression that ambition ruled in his heart, as well as the desire for an easy life. When he meets up with Micah and is offered a job with generous pay, good conditions and little responsibility, he grabs at the chance. The fact that he will serve in an idolatrous shrine, under the power of his benefactor, seems not to trouble him. Indeed when a better offer comes along later (vv. 19–20), he has no compunction in leaving Micah behind to further his own career aspirations.

It is not that ambition, in the sense of wanting to do well, is always wrong. Neither are we suggesting that those called to ministry should live in poverty and poor conditions. They deserve to be cared for and looked after well. What is wrong is that career advancement and personal gain should be the motivation for deciding when and where we should serve God.

Prayer

Lord, thank you for those you have called to serve you. Give them grace to follow you wholeheartedly, wherever you may lead. Amen

TH

A prodigal tribe

In those days Israel had no king. And in those days the tribe of the Danites was seeking a place of their own where they might settle, because they had not yet come into an inheritance among the tribes of Israel. So the Danites sent five warriors from Zorah and Eshtaol to spy out the land and explore it. These men represented all their clans. They told them, 'Go, explore the land.'

Although Joshua had allocated various parts of the promised land to each of the tribes, the conquest remained incomplete because some of the tribes, like the Danites, failed to move forward and take possession of the land God had given them. It was more difficult than they imagined, and they lacked the resolve to bring it about. Tribal weakness forms the third strand in the analysis of Israel's corruption.

As time passed, a second generation emerged who 'knew neither the Lord nor what he had done for Israel' (2:10). They had even less determination and merged with the people around them, largely forgetting their inheritance and their spiritual distinctiveness.

The five warriors seem to typify this spiritual malaise. As the Danites at last stir themselves from their spiritual slumber, they are sent on a reconnaissance mission, but their tactics depend more upon cunning and opportunism than on courage and faith.

First, they look for God's approval at Micah's idolatrous shrine. The compromised priest gladly dispenses a blessing upon them, which they are eager to receive. Second, they choose an easy and defenceless target. The city of Laish stands nearby, a desirable place to live and unprotected. They return to their brethren anxious to launch an attack, even though this is not the territory originally assigned to them.

What a different spirit this is to that of men like Joshua and Caleb! How easy it is to replace faith and courage with human craftiness and worldly methods. How easy it is to depend on manmade religion than on the living God. There will always be a temptation in life to take the easy way out and to find justification for what we do in our religion.

Prayer

Lord, may I never be lacking in spiritual courage, moral integrity and daring faith, no matter how hard it may be. Amen

TH

The weak and the strong

Then six hundred men from the clan of the Danites, armed for battle, set out... When these men went into Micah's house and took the carved image, the ephod, the other household gods and the cast idol, the priest said to them, 'What are you doing?' They answered him, 'Be quiet! Don't say a word. Come with us and be our father and priest.'... When they had gone some distance from Micah's house, the men who lived near Micah were called together and overtook the Danites. As they shouted after them, the Danites turned and said to Micah, 'What's the matter with you that you called out your men to fight?' He replied, 'You took the gods I made, and my priest, and went away. What else do I have?' The Danites answered, 'Don't argue with us, or some hot-tempered men will attack you, and you and your family will lose your lives.'

It is a fine line between assertiveness and aggression. The Danites, roused from their lethargy, cross that line in their shameful treatment of Micah, stealing both his priest and the trappings of his homemade shrine.

From the kindergarten to the boardroom, bullying is a fact of life. The strong and powerful are always tempted to use their power to get what they want. Making sport of those unable to defend themselves gives a perverted kind of pleasure, but is usually a sign of deep insecurity. It has to be opposed wherever it is found, in school, at the workplace, even in church. God is forever on the side of the oppressed, the marginalized and the abused.

The sad incident reveals the inadequacy of Micah's gods. They can do nothing to defend him and are carried away like the useless bits of metal that they are. Betrayed by his priest, his shrine ransacked and empty, his pride humbled by his own powerlessness, Micah returns home a broken man.

We may feel sorry for him, but perhaps there is purpose in his brokenness. Maybe he had to see the futility of his false religion before he could turn again to the true and living God whom he had forsaken in his prosperity and self-confidence. Many a prodigal has discovered that it is the path of brokenness that leads towards home.

Prayer

Lord, protect the weak, and humble the strong. Amen

TH

The false and the true

Then they took what Micah had made, and his priest, and went on to Laish, against a peaceful and unsuspecting people. They attacked them with the sword and burned down their city… The Danites rebuilt the city and settled there. They named it Dan… There the Danites set up for themselves idols, and Jonathan son of Gershom, the son of Moses, and his sons were priests for the tribe of Dan until the time of the captivity of the land. They continued to use the idols Micah had made, all the time the house of God was in Shiloh.

The newly rebuilt city of Dan now becomes the centre of false worship within Israel, a thorn in the side of Israel until the time of the exile. Meanwhile the authentic house of God at Shiloh is ignored and despised.

True religion always has its counterfeit. There will be those who want to water down the demands of genuine faith, lessen its challenge and integrate concepts and ideas that make it more acceptable to the majority. Consequently there is always a struggle between the true and the false. This is why reformers are constantly needed within the Church, to bring us back to the place of true worship and holiness of life.

The apostle Paul fought his own battle with the Judaizers, that group who failed to see that salvation was by faith alone and demanded that Gentiles should follow Jewish customs. Paul resisted fiercely, recognizing that this was not the gospel, but a dangerous muddling of the true message.

Martin Luther fought a similar battle in his own day, rediscovering the truth of justification by faith alone and standing firm against the might of an apostate Church.

Scripture warns us that in the last days 'people will be lovers of themselves, lovers of money, boastful, proud, abusive, disobedient to their parents, ungrateful, unholy… treacherous, rash, conceited, lovers of pleasure rather than lovers of God' (2 Timothy 3:1–5). What is more, they will be 'having a form of godliness but denying its power'.

Therein lies the difference between the true and the false. The false has no power. Only authentic faith carries the anointing of God.

Prayer

Lord, keep us faithful to the truth, protect us from the false and give us wisdom to know the difference. Amen

TH

Moral confusion

In those days Israel had no king. Now a Levite who lived in a remote area in the hill country of Ephraim took a concubine from Bethlehem in Judah. But she was unfaithful to him. She left him and went back of her father's house in Bethlehem, Judah. After she had been there for four months, her husband went to her to persuade her to return... She took him into her father's house, and when her father saw him, he gladly welcomed him. His father-in-law... prevailed upon him to stay; so he remained with him three days, eating and drinking, and sleeping there.

Having seen the religious confusion in Israel, we are now allowed to see the moral chaos in which God's people were living. Again, a Levite is involved.

The unfaithfulness of his concubine (second wife) may refer to adultery or to her leaving him in a fit of rage. Whatever the cause of the breakdown, she returns home. To his credit, and after a suitable 'cooling-off' period, the Levite follows her, seeking reconciliation.

What the story concentrates on, however, is the over-the-top hospitality provided by her father. For three days they eat and drink, which might be considered customary, but he then prevails upon his son-in-law to stay another two days for more of the same. 'Stay tonight and enjoy yourself,' he insists. 'Wait till afternoon!' (vv. 6, 8).

Hedonism is the belief that seeking and experiencing pleasure is the most important thing in life. In itself it seems innocent enough (we all enjoy a good time, don't we?), but the problem is what it can lead to. Today it is a dominant philosophy of many societies, expressed in binge-drinking, drug-taking and casual sex. All too often, religion is painted as straight-laced, oppressive and restrictive of freedom, while those who stand for moral values are ridiculed as puritanical, prudish and out-of-date.

The breakdown of society testifies to the fact that we reap what we sow. Any society without a clear moral framework will eventually implode, as did ancient Rome. It all begins with such seeming innocence.

Prayer

Lord, thank you for the good things you have given us to enjoy. May we do so without losing sight of you or letting go our moral bearings.

TH

Hospitality

[The man, his servant and his concubine] went on, and the sun set as they neared Gibeah in Benjamin. There they stopped to spend the night. They went and sat in the city square, but no one took them into his home for the night. That evening an old man from the hill country of Ephraim, who was living in Gibeah (the men of the place were Benjaminites), came in from his work in the fields... 'You are welcome at my house,' [he] said. 'Let me supply whatever you need. Only don't spend the night in the square.' So he took him into his house and fed his donkeys.

Having been reconciled, the Levite and his concubine eventually prise themselves away from the effusive hospitality of her father, to return home. Travelling past Jebus for the sake of safety, they arrive at Gibeah where they expect to be offered hospitality, but no one bothers with them until an old man comes along.

The old man appears in this grim tale as a light shining in the darkness. He is of an older generation and retains the values and beliefs of a nobler time. His was the generation that entered the land along with Joshua, and they knew the Lord and what he had done for Israel. According to the writer of Judges, the decline in Israel came about partly because the following generation grew up without this kind of living faith (Judges 2:10).

How hard it is to pass on spiritual vitality! Just as those born into wealth seldom appreciate how fortunate they are, so too those born into a spiritual richness often fail to realize how blessed they actually are. It sometimes takes years of painful searching before they come back to their roots.

Generosity of heart is a wonderful, godly quality, which the old man possesses in abundance. Gladly he welcomes the strangers into his home and, amazed to meet fellow Ephraimites, joyfully shares with them whatever he has. Even in the spiritual darkness of these sad times, God has not left himself without a witness. There is a spiritual remnant in Israel.

Simple faithfulness may not be very dramatic, and it may appear insignificant in the face of rampant godlessness, but in the end it will triumph.

Sunday prayer

Lord, in times of darkness and uncertainty, keep us ever faithful.

TH

Think about it! Tell us what to do!

While they were enjoying themselves, some of the wicked men of the city surrounded the house. Pounding on the door, they shouted to the old man who owned the house, 'Bring out the man who came to your house so that we can have sex with him.' The owner of the house went outside and said to them, 'No, my friends, don't be so vile. Since this man is my guest, don't do this disgraceful thing. Look, here is my virgin daughter, and his concubine. I will bring them out to you now, and you can use them and do whatever you wish. But to this man, don't do such a disgraceful thing.' But the men would not listen to him. So the man took his concubine and sent her outside to them.

The quiet enjoyment of an evening at home is suddenly interrupted by the raucous demands of a wild group of evil men intent on homo-sexual rape. This shocking story reveals the depths to which Israel has sunk and the need for someone to stand against it. The only saving feature is that this awful incident becomes a turning point in Israel's history.

The old man's response is a sad mixture of strength and weakness, but who can blame him? What would you have done? That is not to excuse him, but to understand his dilemma. Even good people can be cowards.

The Levite appears callous and unfeeling. The gang rape of his con-cubine, leaving her for dead, appar-ently leaves him unmoved (vv. 27–28). Or is he simply in shock?

Her plight speaks to us of the thousands of women who are devalued, mistreated and abused by men throughout the world. Treated as things to be possessed or objects of sexual gratification, young girls and women are shame-fully treated and cruelly exploited. They have no rights, no voice, no hope. What can be done about it?

As the saying goes, 'All that is necessary for evil to triumph is that good men do nothing'. How true it is! Traumatized by what has taken place the Levite gruesomely cuts up the body and sends a signal to all of Israel (v. 29): 'Enough is enough! Something has to change. What is your response?'

Prayer

Lord, may we not close our eyes to evil. Give us courage to stand up for what is right. Amen

TH

United against the city

Then all the Israelites from Dan to Beersheba and from the land of Gilead came out as one man and assembled before the Lord in Mizpah. The leaders of all the people of the tribes of Israel took their places in the assembly of the people of God, four hundred thousand soldiers armed with swords... Then the Israelites said, 'Tell us how this awful thing happened.'... All the people rose as one man, saying, 'None of us will go home. No, not one of us will return to his house. But now this is what we'll do to Gibeah: We'll go up against it as the lot directs.'... So all the men of Israel got together and united as one man against the city.

It often takes a tragedy before action occurs. Such a thing as happened at Gibeah had never happened before in Israel. There is outrage and anger as the grim details unfold (vv. 4–6).

The tribes come together in a solemn gathering to assess the situation. What surprises us is that there are in fact leaders in Israel. We have had the impression that the situation of moral and religious anarchy has come about because there is no king (and therefore no stable government) and everyone is doing what is right in their own eyes. What we now realize is that the situation has arisen as much because of ineffective leadership. There are leaders in Israel, but they are weak and compromising.

Appropriate confrontation is one of the most difficult aspects of leadership, especially for those of a pastoral nature. It is far easier to turn a blind eye or to sweep things under the carpet than to deal with tricky and painful situations. Unresolved situations don't usually go away. They have a habit of growing more serious and coming back to haunt us. This is what happened in Israel.

It is time for the 'silent majority' to speak up. Israel assembles 'before the Lord' and as the people of God. They have not lost their spiritual identity or their relationship to God despite the spiritual and moral decline. Shocked into response by the realization of the evil in their midst, they are galvanized into action against those responsible for the crime.

Prayer

*Lord, give to all who lead your
people the courage to do what
is right. Amen*

TH

The danger of presumption

Then the Israelites, all the people, went up to Bethel, and there they sat weeping before the Lord. They fasted that day until evening and presented burnt offerings and fellowship offerings to the Lord. And the Israelites enquired of the Lord. (In those days the ark of the covenant of God was there…) They asked, 'Shall we go up again to battle with Benjamin our brother, or not?' The Lord responded, 'Go, for tomorrow I will give them into your hands.'

Motivated by the atrocious behaviour of the men of Gibeah, the Israelites set out to teach them a lesson (see vv. 12–25 for the full story). They presume it will be an easy thing to bring them to justice, but they are tragically mistaken. They fail to take two factors into account. First, the loyalty of the other Benjaminites towards their brethren—they refuse to listen to their request to hand over the perpetrators. Second, the skill of the Benjaminites in fighting—twice they attack, and twice they are soundly beaten. 40,000 men are killed.

There is always a danger of presumption, even when right is on our side. We may be doing a good thing, but if we do it in our own strength, it is likely to fail. Zeal is usually a good quality, but it can be misplaced. Enthusiasm alone is not enough.

God is working even through this shambles, however. Each defeat causes Israel to seek him with even greater sincerity and dependency. Three times they seek the Lord and with growing intensity. In fact what we see in this passage is a mini-revival, a turning to God in the context of repentance and humility. A purging has taken place and not just among the obviously guilty. Israel is being refined. Their weeping reflects a godly sorrow; the sacrifices a dependence upon God's mercy and grace.

We should not assume that doing right will always be easy. We will have to persevere through setbacks, disappointments and sometimes defeats, but God is able to turn our defeats into victory. He can take our failures and brokenness and use them to bring us closer to himself, for it is when we are weak that we are truly strong.

Prayer

Lord, in moments of defeat may I not give up, but depend upon you even more. Amen

TH

Tribal rivalry

On that day twenty-five thousand Benjamite swordsmen fell, all of them valiant fighters. But six hundred men turned and fled into the desert to the rock of Rimmon, where they stayed for four months. The men of Israel went back to Benjamin and put all the town to the sword, including the animals and everything else they found. All the towns they came across they set on fire.

Why such violence? So many things are done in the name of God that clearly are nothing to do with him. One can only assume that the almost wholesale destruction of the tribe of Benjamin was not what God had in mind. Certainly those who committed the crime at Gibeah deserved to be punished accordingly, but the whole tragic incident seems to have spiralled out of control and into a maelstrom of violence and killing, fuelled to a large degree by tribal jealousies.

The stubborn refusal of the Benjamites to give up the guilty parties (v. 13) was clearly wrong, and their unwillingness to listen to fellow Israelites exacerbated an already tense situation. How many conflicts spiral out of control because of misplaced loyalties, inflexible principles and a refusal to hear what the other party is saying?

The Israelites for their part appear to be on a self-righteous 'crusade' to purge Israel of its evil, blinded to their own shortcomings and unwilling to show mercy. Once provoked, their sense of righteous indignation catapults them forward into an extreme overreaction. Again, how the fires of conflict are fuelled by self-righteous zeal and injured pride!

'The Lord defeated Benjamin before Israel' (v. 35). I have to admit that I struggle to understand some of the violence in the Old Testament, especially when it is unprovoked and excessive and seems to be condoned by God. Judged by the standards of the 21st century, it seems gratuitous and out of keeping with the character of God. Perhaps it can only be understood in its own context. Maybe they were acting according to a limited understanding of God. Almost certainly they went beyond what God had intended. It remains problematical, though and, as far as I'm concerned, I'm still thinking it through.

Prayer

Lord, I trust you, even when I can't understand it all. Amen

TH

Why indeed?

The men of Israel had taken an oath at Mizpah: 'Not one of us will give his daughter in marriage to a Benjamite.' The people went to Bethel, where they sat before God until evening, raising their voices and weeping bitterly. 'O Lord, the God of Israel,' they cried, 'why has this happened to Israel? Why should one tribe be missing from Israel today?'… The whole assembly sent an offer of peace to the Benjaminites at the rock of Rimmon… The people grieved for Benjamin, because the Lord had made a gap in the tribes of Israel.

All the tribes of Israel, including Benjamin, have paid a heavy price for the godless behaviour of the men of Gibeah, but also for the years of spiritual neglect that led up to it. Now they come before God to lament the breakdown in national unity and to wonder why they are in such a predicament (as before, read verses 1–21 for the full picture).

It is good to ask the question 'Why?' if it helps us to reflect on our behaviour and learn from our mistakes. Indeed, how will we ever grow if we are unwilling to face up to our shortcomings? It takes courage to do so, but in the presence of God and with the assurance of his forgiving grace, we can be honest with ourselves and deal with the pain that self-awareness often brings, without falling into condemnation.

Unity is a vital factor in church life and, while division is sometimes unavoidable, we should always grieve the loss of fellowship and long for reconciliation. Jesus prayed that we might be one (John 17:21–23), and Paul urges us, in so far as it depends on us, to live at peace with everyone (Romans 12:18).

One stumbling block to Benjamin's restoration is the fact that they have no wives, and the other tribes have rashly vowed not to give their daughters to them in marriage (v. 1). Rather than repent of words spoken in haste, they choose to put into operation an elaborate and questionable strategy involving kidnap by which the Benjaminites can marry (vv. 20–23). It is all a little unsavoury and suggests that the work of refining is not yet complete.

Prayer

Lord, may your people be drawn together, not torn apart. Amen

TH

The need for a king

In those days Israel had no king; everyone did as he saw fit.

And so we return to where we began our studies in Judges, and the book itself closes by repeating the author's analysis of the reason for Israel's plight—there is no king to provide unity and direction and to ensure a strong spiritual dimension to the life of God's people. This will provide the justification for the coming monarchy, which will begin hesitatingly with Saul and find its greatest expression in King David.

I wonder if we can reach beyond the obvious application of these words, and see in the desire for a king a prophetic longing for the one who is the true king of Israel and, indeed, the King of Kings and the Lord of Lords?

In truth only King Jesus can provide the direction that the world today needs. When we survey nations and societies in the 21st century, we can only conclude that, despite advances in science and technology, in many ways modern behaviour is not too dissimilar from that in Israel during the period of the Judges. It makes us cry out in earnest prayer, 'Let your kingdom come, let your will be done, on earth as it is in heaven.'

As Christians we long for the coming of the kingdom of God. It is here in part, but not yet fully, and we long for that day when it will be finally revealed. In the meantime, we can crown Jesus as king in our own lives, give to him the allegiance he so fully deserves and desires and let his kingdom come within us. We can yield ourselves to him in glad obedience, and let his will be done within us. Heaven can touch earth, at least where we are.

Of course governments must do their best to curb antisocial behaviour and the like. As we have seen, we should pray for them and support them in this God-given task. We must never assume that legislation alone can change a person's heart—only God can do that. Society will only be truly transformed when, one by one, we bow the knee to Jesus the King.

Prayer

Lord, let your kingdom come in my heart and your will be done in my life. Amen

TH

Death and resurrection

This is a story about life and death, death and resurrection. John tells it simply but powerfully and movingly, using vivid imagery and presenting us with the conflict of many opposing forces as he covers truth and falsehood, light and dark, fear and courage, doubt and faith, hate and love. He tells us of the difference between going our way and going God's way. He shows us how we can be misled by the way things appear to be, and how God is in control, even in the darkest times, even when there seems to be no hope.

It is a familiar story. You may well be able to recite by heart the course of events of the very few days depicted in these Bible readings. Take the opportunity now to read through John chapters 18—21; listen not just to the events described but also to the way in which John tells them, the journey on which he takes us as we move with Jesus from darkness, powerlessness and death to light, power and resurrection. Walk with the disciples from bewilderment to faith, despair to hope.

Peter is a key character in the story. It is clearly a learning process for him and through him for the rest of us. He learns about submitting to God's will, about not trusting in his own resources. He learns about the importance of belief, about recognizing Jesus, and about the possibility of restoration; he is recommissioned and learns once again to focus on Jesus, not on others. It is all about 'not me, but God' (see John 12:25–26).

So John's account is more than just a story. He has written it down, he tells us, 'that you may believe that Jesus is the Christ, the Son of God, and that by believing you may have life in his name' (John 20:31). Although the events described in these passages cover only a very few days, they are unequalled in significance in the history of the world. As we move through Holy Week to Easter and beyond, the story John tells can make a difference to the way in which we see God at work in the world and in our own life and, as we see what Jesus' death and resurrection meant to John, to Peter, to all the characters we meet in these chapters, we can see more clearly what resurrection means for us.

Jane Cornish

JOHN 18:3–11 (NIV, ABRIDGED)

Walking the Father's way

So Judas came to the grove, guiding a detachment of soldiers and some officials from the chief priests and Pharisees. They were carrying torches, lanterns and weapons. Jesus, knowing all that was going to happen to him, went out and asked them, 'Who is it you want?' 'Jesus of Nazareth,' they replied. 'I am he,' Jesus said. '... If you are looking for me, then let these men go.'... Then Simon Peter, who had a sword, drew it and struck the high priest's servant, cutting off his right ear... Jesus commanded Peter, 'Put your sword away! Shall I not drink the cup the Father has given me?'

Only a few days before, Jesus' disciples had been on top of the world, walking alongside Jesus as he rode into Jerusalem in triumph, the promised Messiah on the brink of claiming his kingdom. Now everything is going wrong. The one they had expected to lead them to victory is being arrested as a common criminal. How can this be part of the plan?

There are times in our lives when events make us wonder what God is doing. Why doesn't he act to put things right? The temptation is to lash out, as Peter does, to try and make sure events go our way. We sulk, threaten, shout, manipulate others and dig our heels in. Like Peter's sword, such weapons would better be put away (v. 11). When life is not going our way, it is more important than ever to listen to what God is saying to us, where he is leading us. Whoever tries to keep his life will lose it and whoever loses his life will preserve it, Jesus told us (Matthew 16:25), and not only did he tell us this, he demonstrated that it was true.

We may not die for our faith but we will at some point have to let go of cherished hopes, ambitions and the way we planned to do things. God's way is best, even if it is not always comfortable. So it is that, as Jesus submits to his father's will, it is he, not Peter with his sword, nor even the large, armed arresting power, whom we see to be in control of the situation.

Sunday prayer

*Lord, teach me the right way to act,
and the right time to refrain
from action.*

JC

JOHN 18:17–18, 25–27 (NIV, ABRIDGED)

Moment of truth

'You are not one of his disciples, are you?' the girl at the door asked Peter. He replied, 'I am not.' It was cold, and the servants and officials stood round a fire they had made to keep warm. Peter also was standing with them, warming himself… he was asked, 'You are not one of his disciples, are you?' He denied it, saying, 'I am not.' One of the high priest's servants, a relative of the man whose ear Peter had cut off, challenged him, 'Didn't I see you with him in the olive grove?' Again Peter denied it, and at that moment a cock began to crow.

Three times Peter denies knowing Jesus, but, as the cock crows, the lies all lead up to a profound moment of truth. Peter realizes he is not quite the rock he thought. He has had to learn a lot in one night. All he wanted was to follow Jesus and serve him, but his efforts have not turned out as he intended. First he refused to let Jesus wash his feet (John 13:8) and was rebuked for that; he tried to defend Jesus in the garden, and again it turned out to be the wrong action to take; now, after following Jesus to the high priest's house (something that must have taken a great deal of courage), he finds that his earlier intention to follow Jesus even to death (13:27) proves hollow, as he panics and denies even knowing him.

There is obviously nothing wrong with being keen to serve Jesus! What Peter—like all of us—has to realize is that our own resources are never enough. Only when we come to the end of relying on ourselves and learn, as Peter learns here, that our love, our faith, our courage and good intentions are not enough to carry us through, do we truly come to depend on Jesus and look to him for everything we need. If there is a sort of death in realizing our own neediness, there is certainly a new, liberating life in knowing that God accepts us just as we are and gives us all the resources he wants us to use in his service.

Reflection and prayer

Are there times when you need to be more willing to stand up for Jesus? Ask God for his help in those situations.

JC

Taking sides

Pilate then went back inside the palace, summoned Jesus and asked him, 'Are you the king of the Jews?'... Jesus said, 'My kingdom is not of this world. If it were, my servants would fight to prevent my arrest by the Jews. But now my kingdom is from another place.' 'You are a king, then!' said Pilate. Jesus answered, 'You are right in saying I am a king. In fact, for this reason I was born, and for this I came into the world, to testify to the truth. Everyone on the side of truth listens to me.' 'What is truth?' Pilate asked. With this he went out again to the Jews and said, 'I find no basis for a charge against him.'

This is a trial that Pilate does not want. He has already suggested that it is nothing to do with him (v. 31) but Jesus' accusers insist. A man who calls himself king could be a threat to Rome, of course, but Jesus' answer to his question confirms in Pilate's mind that the whole matter is a waste of time. What does it matter if Jesus calls himself a king if he doesn't intend to fight the establishment? Pilate probably sees him less as a revolutionary than as yet another religious fanatic. He seems, to Pilate, to change the subject when he starts talking about truth, because truth is irrelevant to the sort of kingship Pilate knows.

What is truth? Pilate was probably more dismissive than enquiring. Jesus' kingdom and values are indeed another world to him; he is more interested in what is helpful and profitable than what is true.

He is not alone. The whole trial shows how far Jesus' concern for the truth is removed from the values of those around him. There are indeed two kingdoms here, two sets of values clashing. One defends itself by power and force (v. 36); the other knows that there is a higher power to whom all will answer.

Like Pilate, each one of us faces a choice about which kingdom we belong to. Commitment to the truth can be costly as it comes into conflict with the interests of others and indeed may go against our own self-interest—but it is part of following the true king.

Reflection

What does it mean to me to be 'on the side of truth' (v. 37)?

JC

JOHN 19:7–15 (NIV, ABRIDGED)

Faith or fear?

The Jews insisted, 'We have a law, and according to that law he must die, because he claimed to be the Son of God.' When Pilate heard this, he was even more afraid, and he went back inside the palace. 'Where do you come from?' he asked Jesus, but Jesus gave him no answer. 'Do you refuse to speak to me?' Pilate said. 'Don't you realize I have power either to free you or to crucify you?' Jesus answered, 'You would have no power over me if it were not given to you from above.'... From then on, Pilate tried to set Jesus free, but the Jews kept shouting, 'If you let this man go, you are no friend of Caesar. Anyone who claims to be a king opposes Caesar.'... 'Shall I crucify your king?' Pilate asked. 'We have no king but Caesar,' the chief priests answered.

Truth having been dismissed as an issue, the trial now revolves around questions of power and manipulation. Pilate is afraid—of becoming involved in a religious argument, but even more of Caesar. He finds no case against Jesus (v. 6) but fear drives his decisions. He wants to inspire that same fear in Jesus (v. 10), but Jesus knows that neither Pilate, nor Caesar, but God is the ultimate authority, and this is reflected in his words and actions.

Jesus' accusers, meanwhile, are using Pilate's fear to manipulate him. They have manufactured this bizarre trial in which Pilate is going in and out of his headquarters, interrogating Jesus inside and then speaking to them outside, because they wished 'to avoid ritual defilement' (18:28). The irony is clear. They are bringing false charges, sending Jesus to an undeserved death for reasons of expediency, but think they can stay ritually clean! When all else fails they deny their allegiance to God by claiming to have no king but Caesar (19:12). No wonder Jesus had accused such people of hypocrisy: outwardly righteous but inwardly scheming (Matthew 23:28).

Fear makes us act defensively, lashing out at others or going behind their backs. It leaves us open to manipulation by the unscrupulous and by those with fears of their own. If we believe that God is in charge, we will be more likely to do what we know to be right.

Prayer

Ask God to help you overcome your fears and trust him more.

JC

The sign

So the soldiers took charge of Jesus. Carrying his own cross, he went out to the place of the Skull (which in Aramaic is called Golgotha). Here they crucified him, and with him two others—one on each side and Jesus in the middle. Pilate had a notice prepared and fastened to the cross. It read: JESUS OF NAZARETH, THE KING OF THE JEWS. Many of the Jews read this sign, for the place where Jesus was crucified was near the city, and the sign was written in Aramaic, Latin and Greek. The chief priests of the Jews protested to Pilate, 'Do not write "The King of the Jews", but that this man claimed to be king of the Jews.' Pilate answered, 'What I have written, I have written.'

Having given in over the crucifixion of Jesus, Pilate decides to take a firm stand over the sign on the cross. In a sense it is a futile gesture: being tough over the trivial while showing weakness in areas that really matter. In this sign, however, displayed for all to see, is the truth Pilate refused to uphold or even acknowledge as a meaningful reality during the trial. Jesus is the 'King of the Jews'.

The chief priests are horrified, of course—the sign reads less like an accusation of crime than an indictment of their judgment. Against their claim to have no king but Caesar, against their protestations of blasphemy this truth is written up there. Like a proclamation of victory lifted high above the heads of his accusers, Jesus is defined as King of the Jews. Of course his kingdom stretches even further than this (10:16). The three languages in which the sign is written together spanned all the countries of the region, as well as the whole of the Roman empire—to those present, it was there for the whole 'world' to see.

As the trial comes to an end with an apparent victory for appeasement and compromise, truth is there at the centre of the whole event for those who choose to pay attention. It always is.

Reflection

Everything we do bears witness to the truth about who we are, and what we really believe, whether we mean it to or not. What message can people read from our lives?

JC

JOHN 19:28–35 (NIV, ABRIDGED)

Turning point

Later, knowing that all was now completed, and so that the Scripture would be fulfilled, Jesus said, 'I am thirsty.' A jar of wine vinegar was there, so they soaked a sponge in it... and lifted it to Jesus' lips. When he had received the drink, Jesus said, 'It is finished.' With that, he bowed his head and gave up his spirit... when they came to Jesus and found that he was already dead, they did not break his legs. Instead, one of the soldiers pierced Jesus' side with a spear, bringing a sudden flow of blood and water. The man who saw it has given testimony, and his testimony is true. He knows that he tells the truth, and he testifies so that you also may believe.

The familiarity of the Gospel accounts, together with their straightforward, understated way of describing the crucifixion, can hide the horror of it all. This is an eye-witness account of the agonizing and humiliating death of a close friend and the end of his followers' hopes. We know now that death was followed by resurrection; although that changes the whole picture, it should not, as we consider what Jesus did for us, detract from the reality of the death. Jesus' sacrifice, conveyed so simply and directly in John's account, was costly.

At the same time the very moment of death was the moment of victory for, as Jesus dies, he declares, 'It is finished.' The Greek word is one that would have been used on a bill that was fully paid. Jesus' death is not the failure of his mission, but its completion—as he died he knew that he had accomplished what he came to do. His work is finished and a new era has begun in which sin and death have been defeated and we can be reconciled to God.

In freely giving himself to do God's will, Jesus shows us a better way of living than the fear and self-interest that have dominated the events of the past few days, that dominate far too many events in our world, and has opened the way back to God.

Reflection

John knows that he has an important truth to pass on and the same commission is given to all who have come to know Jesus' truth. This Easter, don't keep it to yourself!

JC

JOHN 19:38–42 (NIV, ABRIDGED)

The in-between time

Later, Joseph of Arimathea asked Pilate for the body of Jesus. Now Joseph was a disciple of Jesus, but secretly because he feared the Jews. With Pilate's permission, he came and took the body away. He was accompanied by Nicodemus, the man who earlier had visited Jesus at night. Nicodemus brought a mixture of myrrh and aloes, about seventy-five pounds. Taking Jesus' body, the two of them wrapped it, with the spices, in strips of linen... At the place where Jesus was crucified, there was a garden, and in the garden a new tomb, in which no one had ever been laid. Because it was the Jewish day of Preparation and since the tomb was nearby, they laid Jesus there.

Here we meet two disciples very different from Peter: anything but impulsive. Joseph has been a secret disciple, because of the consequences that openly following Jesus would have had. Nicodemus, too, came to Jesus at night (ch. 3), in order to keep his interest quiet. Now, when all seems lost and there is surely nothing to be gained by revealing their loyalties, they ask for Jesus' body.

Sometimes we may wonder what we are achieving as we struggle on in our Christian service. Keeping going in a dwindling congregation, our worship and witness ignored by the community at large; living out our faith in a society that makes light of our values and ridicules the good news we are offering can seem as futile and empty a gesture as declaring our allegiance after the crucifixion or committing a large amount of costly spices to burying the body of an apparently failed leader.

The time between death and resurrection can seem the most hopeless time of all. Like winter, when everything seems dead, but under the snow the bulbs are preparing to grow again and the apparently lifeless trees will burst into leaf at the right moment. In the same way God's plan is at work in the world even when nothing appears to be happening. God's call to us is to carry on faithfully, even when we cannot see what he is doing. We can be sure that he has a purpose and, if we are faithful, it will be fulfilled in our lives.

Prayer

Ask God to help you keep going even when there is no sign of life.

JC

JOHN 20:1–9 (NIV, ABRIDGED)

Resurrection

Early on the first day of the week, while it was still dark, Mary Magdalene went to the tomb and saw that the stone had been removed from the entrance. So she came running to Simon Peter and the other disciple, the one Jesus loved, and said, 'They have taken the Lord out of the tomb, and we don't know where they have put him!' So Peter and the other disciple started for the tomb… Simon Peter… arrived and went into the tomb. He saw the strips of linen lying there, as well as the burial cloth that had been around Jesus' head. The cloth was folded up by itself, separate from the linen. Finally the other disciple… also went inside. He saw and believed. (They still did not understand from Scripture that Jesus had to rise from the dead.)

In some ways it's a strangely muted account of such a wonderful event. Instead of joy, we read an account of shock, confusion and only tentative belief. As we move from death to resurrection, it is still dark (v. 1)—dawn has not yet arrived, neither has light yet dawned in the disciples' minds. Mary takes one look and jumps to the obvious conclusion; Peter examines the evidence a bit more; the other disciple believed, though without understanding.

What did he believe? It is difficult to say, but it seems likely that he is at least willing to trust God when the evidence does not add up. Perhaps the whole scene reminded them of a grave they had seen earlier that year when Lazarus, dead three days, came out in response to Jesus' call (ch. 11).

Faith is not about having all the answers. It is 'being sure of what we hope for and certain of what we do not see' (Hebrews 11:1). Whether we have recently come to know Christ or have been a Christian for our whole life, there will always be questions. Our journey to new life in Christ is not a matter of overnight transformation ,but a process that lasts a lifetime. One thing is certain—for these disciples, and for us, things will never be the same again if we are open to God's transforming power.

Easter prayer

Praise God for the resurrection, and the new life he brings each one of us in Christ.

JC

Meeting Jesus

Mary stood outside the tomb crying. As she wept, she bent over to look into the tomb and saw two angels in white, seated where Jesus' body had been, one at the head and the other at the foot. They asked her, 'Woman, why are you crying?' 'They have taken my Lord away,' she said, 'and I don't know where they have put him.' At this, she turned round and saw Jesus standing there, but she did not realize that it was Jesus. 'Woman,' he said, 'why are you crying? Who is it you are looking for?' Thinking he was the gardener, she said, 'Sir, if you have carried him away, tell me where you have put him, and I will get him.' Jesus said to her, 'Mary.' She turned towards him and cried out in Aramaic, 'Rabboni!' (which means Teacher).

A new day has dawned, a new era begun—the most momentous event in the history of the world has happened, but there was no blinding flash of light, no fanfare. For Mary nothing has changed. Overwhelmed by the events of the last few days and the unexpected turn events have taken, she stands crying. Through her tears she does not realize who is standing next to her.

Grief is a very isolating experience. Laugh and the world laughs with you, goes the saying, cry and you weep alone. When we grieve we can easily feel that nobody understands, nobody wants to know. Even those who care seem powerless to reach out and touch us in our need. Often, in the midst of grief, we wonder where God is. Just as Mary was unaware of Jesus'

presence, God is there with us in our pain, whether we recognize him or not. He speaks our name and calls us to new life.

Until we turn and see Jesus, we will not know the joy of resurrection. For some people this happens as an overwhelming conversion experience; for others, like Mary, the light dawns gradually. But it is not a one-off event for any of us. We need to turn to Jesus day after day, to look to him to meet us at times of celebration and in times of grief, and to allow him to lead us into each new day.

Prayer

As you come to Jesus today, allow his presence to transform your life.

JC

Inheritance

On the evening of that first day of the week, when the disciples were together, with the doors locked for fear of the Jews, Jesus came and stood among them and said, 'Peace be with you!' After he said this, he showed them his hands and side. The disciples were overjoyed when they saw the Lord. Again Jesus said, 'Peace be with you! As the Father has sent me, I am sending you.' And with that he breathed on them and said, 'Receive the Holy Spirit. If you forgive anyone his sins, they are forgiven; if you do not forgive them, they are not forgiven.'

The night is past, death has done its worst and yet resurrection has happened. It sounds like the ultimate in happy endings—except that this is far from the end. To begin with, the disciples are still in danger. The authorities are not happy at the disappearance of Jesus' body, at the rumours that are beginning to fly round, and the disciples are guilty by association. Who knows what will happen to them?

At the same time they have heard the rumours themselves. Would Jesus come and put everything right? Perhaps he would at last fulfil their expectations and prove to be the Messiah that they had been expecting; now the kingdom would be restored and he would claim the throne.

When Jesus finally does appear, they are filled with joy (v. 20), but his message to them is not what they might have expected. There is still work to be done (v. 21) and Jesus is sending them to fulfil the task.

He is not, however, leaving them to do it in their own strength. He gives them the Holy Spirit; he equips them with power for the task to which he calls them. Even so, the task remains. Jesus does not come into our lives to put everything right, to make it all easy. He comes to send us—equipped by his Spirit—to be fellow workers, to continue the work for which he came. Knowing Jesus and the power of his resurrection will not make our lives comfortable, but in his power we can witness to the joy, peace and forgiveness he offers us, even when circumstances are far from easy.

Prayer

Ask God to equip you for the task he has given you.

JC

Knowing and believing

Now Thomas (called Didymus), one of the Twelve, was not with the disciples when Jesus came. So the other disciples told him, 'We have seen the Lord!' But he said to them, 'Unless I see the nail marks in his hands and put my finger where the nails were, and put my hand into his side, I will not believe it.' A week later his disciples were in the house again, and Thomas was with them. Though the doors were locked, Jesus came and stood among them and said, 'Peace be with you!' Then he said to Thomas, 'Put your finger here; see my hands. Reach out your hand and put it into my side. Stop doubting and believe.' Thomas said to him, 'My Lord and my God!'

As John has taken us through the events of the past few days, we have seen that things are not always as they seem. Strength has been found in apparent powerlessness; lies have revealed truth; death has been the way to life. But is the resurrection really what it seems? The disciples claim to have seen the Lord, but one short resurrection appearance is very little on which to stake your whole life. Thomas wants more proof.

There are right and wrong types of scepticism. The scientist rightly puts everything to the test, believing nothing that cannot be verified by experiment. When it comes to trusting the people we love, demanding proof of their word can be a sign that the relationship is in trouble. So it is that Thomas, who cannot believe in the abstract, is won over by the mere presence of Christ before him, his Lord and his God. Our Christian faith is not a matter of believing against all the evidence, but at the same time we know that we do not always have the full picture, and sometimes we have to trust God without demanding proof.

As we saw at the beginning of these readings, John wrote about Jesus not merely as a biography of someone he admired, but because he wanted his readers to believe in something that was worth staking their lives on. Thomas, the sceptic who was won round by Jesus helps us to see that here is truth—credible and worth believing.

Prayer

Worship Jesus as your Lord and your God.

JC

Recognizing Jesus

Early in the morning, Jesus stood on the shore, but the disciples did not realize that it was Jesus. He called out to them, 'Friends, haven't you any fish?' 'No,' they answered. He said, 'Throw your net on the right side of the boat and you will find some.' When they did, they were unable to haul the net in because of the large number of fish. Then the disciple whom Jesus loved said to Peter, 'It is the Lord!'... When they landed, they saw a fire of burning coals there with fish on it, and some bread... Jesus said to them, 'Come and have breakfast.' None of the disciples dared ask him, 'Who are you?' They knew it was the Lord.

There was something different about Jesus. While the disciples did not know him immediately, in the end there was no mistaking him. When we know someone well we recognize them so readily that we don't need to look at the signature at the bottom of the letter, the name on the gift tag or to ask who it was that performed that helpful job. Their signature is, as it were, all over the act. So it is with Jesus. That's how they knew it was Jesus on the shore, even before they got to land. He has helped them with fishing before (Luke 5:1–7) and he has shared food with them. They know the person, even if he is somehow not exactly the same.

How do we recognize Jesus today? We can't go by looks because he is not physically here. Yet, like the disciples, we know he is with us. We recognize Jesus in our lives by the familiar action, the loving gesture, the caring touch. We recognize him in other people who care for us in his name. We recognize him in that inspiration to 'throw our nets out on the other side', to do something differently, which suddenly transforms our situation. Yet, like the disciples, we are constantly surprised, finding as we walk with him that he is never quite what we expect. He calls us to see him afresh, to follow him into new ventures and meet him in the most unexpected people and places.

Prayer

Lord, help me to recognize your presence with me today. Thank you for your care and your call.

JC

Recommissioning

When they had finished eating, Jesus said to Simon Peter, 'Simon son of John, do you truly love me more than these?' 'Yes, Lord,' he said, 'you know that I love you.' Jesus said, 'Feed my lambs.' Again Jesus said, 'Simon son of John, do you truly love me?' He answered, 'Yes, Lord, you know that I love you.' Jesus said, 'Take care of my sheep.' The third time he said to him, 'Simon son of John, do you love me?' Peter was hurt because Jesus asked him the third time, 'Do you love me?' He said, 'Lord, you know all things; you know that I love you.' Jesus said, 'Feed my sheep...' Then he said to him, 'Follow me!'

Just as the fishing incident reminds us of an earlier occasion by a lake, so now the breakfast round the fire must have reminded Peter of another fire, only a few nights before. Then it had seemed like the end of the world; now the disciples have new hope and confidence as death has been overturned by resurrection. Then Peter denied Jesus; now he has no hesitation in answering Jesus' question positively (v. 15)—but by the third time Jesus asks, he is hurt.

Does Jesus doubt him? Of course he doesn't; he knows the answer, as Peter says (v. 17). Three times Peter had denied that love, and three times Jesus asks him to affirm it. For Peter, as well as for Jesus, resurrection does not mean taking up the old life again, but a fresh start, putting past mistakes behind him and not merely ignoring or glossing over them.

Whatever we have done, God always calls us afresh. In this story of death and resurrection there have been many second chances: the bread of friendship offered to Judas at the last moment (13:26), Pilate's chance to know truth and his offer to release Jesus that gave the priests the opportunity to draw back from their actions, but the chances were not taken. Like Peter, we need to move forward with Jesus, not defined by the past but willing to listen to God and move on through repentance to resurrection life.

Reflection

'Do you love me?' Jesus asks us all to answer this question; not just in what we say, but by how we live.

JC

Keeping focused

Peter turned and saw that the disciple whom Jesus loved was following them... When Peter saw him, he asked, 'Lord, what about him?' Jesus answered, 'If I want him to remain alive until I return, what is that to you? You must follow me.' Because of this, the rumour spread among the brothers that this disciple would not die. But Jesus did not say that he would not die; he only said, 'If I want him to remain alive until I return, what is that to you?' This is the disciple who testifies to these things and who wrote them down. We know that his testimony is true. Jesus did many other things as well. If every one of them were written down, I suppose that even the whole world would not have room for the books that would be written.

There are times when we just want to take the spotlight off ourselves. From the earliest records of humanity, the tendency has been to try and put somebody else centre-stage when in a difficult situation (see, for example, Genesis 3:12–13). Peter has been challenged to follow Jesus whatever the cost. His immediate reaction is to ask if Jesus is demanding the same of others but, as Jesus tells him, that is not the point. He is not going to tell him about others—only what he is asking of him.

Each person's path is different. Being called to follow Christ will not mean the same for you as it does for me or the person who sits next to you in church. Comparing ourselves to others just leads to resentment, smugness, despair or guilt. As we come to the end of these readings in John's Gospel we have seen what walking God's way meant for Jesus. What it will mean for us, as we commit anew each day to follow Jesus, we cannot know; but we can know that God is in charge, as he has been throughout the events we have been following. In the end his is the only way to go.

Reflection

The Gospel ends with an assurance that John's testimony is true (v. 25). As those people who have 'not seen and yet have come to believe' (20:29), what testimony can we give to what we have seen Jesus doing in our lives?

JC

Psalms of life: 107—150

The book of Psalms, perhaps more so than any other part of the Bible, gives us permission to be real. There can be a tendency in Christian circles to expect of ourselves and others that we always and only praise God and do not express doubts, fears, anger, despair or any other negative emotion or frame of mind. This expectation is a denial of the reality of the life of faith and leads at best to a deformed kind of spiritual growth. It may lead to total loss of faith in those who feel condemned as they fail to live up to these supposed exalted standards. I am eternally grateful that I had learned to view this approach to the Christian's walk with God with great scepticism before I entered a very dark period of my life a few years ago. Had I not, I too would have been a casualty.

John Calvin, writing in the sixteenth century, called the book of Psalms 'An Anatomy of all the Parts of the Soul' and explained, 'for there is not an emotion of which anyone can be conscious that is not here represented as in a mirror.' This does not mean that we have permission to have a negative view of life in this world or to indulge in self-pity.

The point of the psalms is that we address God and acknowledge his activity in all of life and his purposes as ultimately fulfilled, no matter how chaotic things may seem at the present time. The psalms of praise, especially those that come after a great deliverance, are the model to which we should always aspire and in pouring out any negative thoughts to God it must be with this intention. We come as those who do not understand to the one who does, seeking enlightenment, the strength to carry on in faith and a growth towards maturity. In this way we join with God in the battle against the evils of this world and enter into his victory over them.

Over these two weeks we shall look at a variety of psalms. We shall learn from those which express the faith that everything in the garden is lovely, as well as from those which express a sense of total disaster and impending doom, and we shall have the opportunity to stand on the heights of victory as God is seen as our saviour and deliverer.

Anne Roberts

Psalm 145:1–3, 8–17 (NIV, abridged)

Awesome but tender

I will exalt you, my God the King; I will praise your name for ever and ever. Every day I will praise you and extol your name for ever and ever. Great is the Lord and most worthy of praise; his greatness no one can fathom... The Lord is gracious and compassionate, slow to anger and rich in love... The Lord is faithful to all his promises and loving towards all he has made. The Lord is righteous in all his ways and loving towards all he has made.

The psalm opens by setting God in his place over the whole of creation. His works are mighty and awesome, his greatness unfathomable and words cannot convey the splendour of his majesty. How far removed and unapproachable such a God could be. The greatest wonder of all is that he is not! Graciousness and compassion, love and goodness are as much a part of his nature as is his glory.

The lines of the poem begin with each letter of the alphabet in sequence, a poetic device that emphasizes the order of God's creation and the totality of his reign. Each verse of the poem (as opposed to the verses in our Bible) opens with a statement of one or more of God's attributes—greatness (our v. 3), graciousness and compassion (v. 8), faithfulness (v. 13) and righteousness and love (v. 17). The great and mighty God is in covenant relationship with his people. He holds everything together for their benefit. There is nothing he cannot and will not do to secure their well-being, and this is not just theory. God's people together celebrate their experience of many tokens of his faithful love. They know him to be utterly reliable.

Here is some of the meaning of Jesus' words, 'I tell you the truth, unless you change and become like little children, you will never enter the kingdom of heaven' (Matthew 18:3). Suspicion, fear and rebellion will keep us effectively outside the kingdom. It is not that faith guarantees an easy ride, but when we fall, God takes us by the hand and raises us up as would a parent a child. He uses his awesome power to demonstrate his tender love.

Sunday reflection

Let the greatness of God in all his attributes inspire your worship.

AR

Wealth without worry

Blessed is the man who fears the Lord, who finds great delight in his commands. His children will be mighty in the land; the generation of the upright will be blessed... Good will come to him who is generous and lends freely, who conducts his affairs with justice. Surely he will never be shaken; a righteous man will be remembered for ever. He will have no fear of bad news; his heart is steadfast, trusting in the Lord. His heart is secure, he will have no fear; in the end he will look in triumph on his foes.

This psalm describes the experience of some believers. Not everyone 'who finds great delight in his commands' produces brilliant children or piles up riches that are the envy of the neighbourhood. It is the practice of Old Testament writers to see everything as attributable to God in some way or having some very close relationship to faith in him or lack of it. Thus where a wealthy man with perfect children is one who worships God and obeys him, his success is seen as directly attributable to that worship and obedience.

Of course, there is more to it than that. A person who is generous and who lends without worrying about the certainty of repayment has a right approach to wealth. He is not stashing it away for his own benefit or spending sleepless nights worrying about his investments. If his ship fails to come in, he himself is not shipwrecked but continues to trust in God who gave him his wealth in the first place. If his enemies gloat over his misfortune that is nothing to him because what they suppose to be his downfall is not, in fact, since his happiness did not consist in his wealth but in giving it away.

In so far as we are successful or wealthy, we should attribute that to God, provided of course that we have gained that success by godly means and in obedience to him. If we are overly worried about our continued success, perhaps we could find peace in sharing what we have with those less fortunate and our joy in a fairer distribution of wealth, which is more often down to us than to God.

Prayer

Father God, we praise you as one who gives generously. Help us to be imitators of your generous heart.

AR

Seeing straight

Praise the Lord, O my soul… He wraps himself in light as with a garment; he stretches out the heavens like a tent… He makes the clouds his chariot and rides on the wings of the wind. He makes winds his messengers, flames of fire his servants. He set the earth on its foundations; it can never be moved… He makes grass grow for the cattle, and plants for man to cultivate—bringing forth food from the earth: wine that gladdens the heart of man, oil to make his face shine, and bread that sustains his heart.

The earth quakes; volcanoes erupt; sinners sin (v. 32, 35), but today, from the psalmist's perspective, all is well. The things that spoil are far removed—today. And on such a day it is right to give all the glory to God. It is a day when the soul should sing and it is easy to do so.

The psalm gives a pre-scientific account of how our world came into being, but that does not negate its relevance for us. Its function is to deal with any tendency to worship the creature rather than the Creator. God is firmly set in place on the throne. By whatever means and over however long a period of time, he was and still is responsible for the created world. We can attach so much importance to accumulating the fruits of creation that the giver of all good things all but disappears from our worldview. The psalm rebukes these unhelpful traits.

Nevertheless we are to enjoy the works of God's hands. As I travel to college over Lancashire's West Pennine moors, I am strengthened by their beauty. Travelling home, problems recede as my attention is drawn by the hills and ever-changing skies. I am not escaping from reality. I cannot wave a magic wand and heal the world of 16-year-olds who live alone or who abuse their bodies with heavy drinking, drugs or casual sex, but I can rightly regain a God-centred perspective with the help of his awesome creation. The psalm reassures us of God's loving provision for all his creatures, acknowledged or not.

Prayer

Creator God, we worship you as we see your beauty and majesty reflected in the works of creation and experience your bountiful care.

AR

Differences need not divide

How good and pleasant it is when brothers live together in unity! It is like precious oil poured on the head, running down on the beard, running down on Aaron's beard, down upon the collar of his robes. It is as if the dew of Hermon were falling on Mount Zion. For there the Lord bestows his blessing, even life for evermore.

The precious and expensive oil of priestly anointing was used without sparing. The dew of Mount Hermon saturates the ground. When people—families, fellowships, groups of friends—meet and share God's love there is a sense of his abundant provision. Differences do not divide, but add to the occasion. Unity comes as we rejoice in what he has done in our individual lives and for us as a body.

At times of national rejoicing differences of politics, faith or economic standing fall away. A church building project is completed or we gather to pray for a group going off on a mission—and we are one in purpose, earlier differences forgotten. On special family occasions our attention is on those being married or whose birthday it is or whose death we mourn, and past quarrels are of no consequence.

That, of course, is the ideal, but if we do not believe it can happen, we may be sure it will not. It is imperative that we learn to rejoice in difference, forgiving and being forgiven, and show the world that

God does provide, pointing to him and not in accusation at each other.

I remember once asking a 17-year-old student what she was doing on Christmas Day. Perhaps I should have known better. Her mother regularly takes off and leaves her and her younger brother without food or money. She said she would probably be alone—'I don't think my mother will be there.'

I spend Christmas each year with family and friends and I am reminded that those of us who have the opportunity of togetherness in Christ and of sharing his love must realize how blessed we are and cover our differences with love. It is 'there' in his will, which is Mount Zion, that he gives us his blessing which will overflow—like the oil—to those in need.

Prayer

Our one God, help us to remember that we are one, the fruits of your creative love.

AR

Growing up

My heart is not proud, O Lord, my eyes are not haughty; I do not concern myself with great matters or things too wonderful for me. But I have stilled and quieted my soul; like a weaned child with its mother, like a weaned child is my soul within me. O Israel, put your hope in the Lord both now and for evermore.

The testimony here is of a person totally submitted to God's will and satisfied with it. To today's thinking it may sound obsequious, mindless, overly dependent, such is the reaction to virtues once valued, and commended throughout God's word.

It is vital to our understanding of this psalm that we discern the type of dependence it expresses. It is not a matter of submission to a despot who demands unquestioning allegiance. Neither is it dependence on a mother, spouse or friend who is prepared to take on all the responsibility within the relationship, providing a cushion against the real world.

It is the dependence of the child who has been nourished at her mother's breast and now moves independently through the world sustained by her mother's continuing love and total acceptance. Maternal love, properly expressed, has inspired absolute trust and confidence. It models a relationship in which another knows what is best for us and may be depended upon entirely.

As reality hits home, life beyond the cradle begins to hurt and puzzle and disappoint; everything is out of joint and the world wobbles on its axis, yet there is an enduring trust and a confidence that one day all will be well. Only with this underlying confidence can faith remain afloat in the storms of life. We may shout our protest, hurl our questions and express our anger precisely because we have this relationship but cannot square it with what is happening. We cling on, sometimes by the skin of our teeth, and refuse to be deceived by appearances. It is this kind of faith that underlies the group of psalms we shall look at from tomorrow as we see the child becoming an adult.

Prayer

Dear Lord, thank you that motherly love has its origins in you. Thank you that your love never fails and that I may depend upon you utterly. Help me never to lose my first love but to grow up in it.

AR

Being real

Out of the depths I cry to you, O Lord; O Lord, hear my voice. Let your ears be attentive to my cry for mercy. If you, O Lord, kept a record of sins, O Lord, who could stand? But with you there is forgiveness; therefore you are feared. I wait for the Lord, my soul waits, and in his word I put my hope. My soul waits for the Lord more than watchmen wait for the morning, more then watchmen wait for the morning.

I cannot remember ever reading a book about prayer that taught me how to pray a prayer of lament. In the Psalms, however, we find a raw honesty, a willingness to question, even to challenge God. In most church traditions we may choose which psalms we use, or refuse to use, in worship. We may then deny ourselves a resource that takes us into the depths of human experience, where we learn to know God as well as, if not better than, when we are on the mountain tops of life.

Here in Psalm 130 the mourner does not doubt the existence of God; he simply wonders if God is listening any longer. There is a sense of sin, but that cannot keep God from remedying the situation because he does not hold our sins against us. All the psalmist can do is wait. God has promised good, so good will come, but probably not yet.

A business partner of my husband was going through a difficult time and he was taking it out on my husband. He did not mean to, but he was wearing my husband down. I did not do it very lovingly, I am afraid, but I rang and told him that my husband could not take any more. The partner said he wanted to 'smash someone's face in.' I said he should take his feelings out on God, because he could take it and we couldn't.

Psalms like this one give us permission to express anger to God and tell him that we doubt his goodness or at least that we don't believe he's good to us any longer, however much he may favour others.

Prayer

Compassionate God, when we pass through the vale of tears, may we learn that you weep with us.

AR

It's all right to grieve

By the rivers of Babylon we sat and wept when we remembered Zion... How can we sing the songs of the Lord while in a foreign land? If I forget you, O Jerusalem, may my right hand forget its skill. May my tongue cling to the roof of my mouth if I do not remember you... O Daughter of Babylon, doomed to destruction, happy is he who repays you for what you have done to us—he who seizes your infants and dashes them against the rocks.

Some churches occasionally hold a Service of Lament—over the sin that destroys; over tsunamis and hurricanes and earthquakes. Why should we deny their existence when we go through the church doors, perhaps recalling them only in a prayer of intercession for the needs of the world?

Once a year my (Anglican) church holds a memorial service for all who have had a bereavement over the past 12 months. The grief is shared and the hymns praise God as our loving Father, holding out the hope of eternal life. It is very well attended by those who do not normally come to church.

If we deny darkness as part of the Christian life, insisting that it is only our perspective which needs changing, we are trying to live on another planet. Was Jesus' perspective wrong when he sweated blood in Gethsemane or when he cried out, 'My God, my God, why have you forsaken me'? Earthly reality includes darkness, even the dark-ness of sometimes wishing terrible things for our enemies and their children as we struggle to make sense of what is happening.

In exile in Babylon there were those who did not forget Jerusalem. Their refusal to forget the God whose temple was back there made Babylon such a dark place for them. They chose to stay with the dark-ness, refusing to intermarry and live a comfortable life in the most advanced civilization of the time. The darkness was such that they wished the worst for their enemies. They could ask God their ques-tions, issue their challenge and stay around to hear the answer. This kind of dialogue is the road to a mature understanding of the life of faith.

Prayer

Loving God, thank you that you promise to comfort us and dry our tears, however much we may weep and rage.

AR

Hope in despair

O Lord, hear my prayer, listen to my cry for mercy; in your faithfulness and righteousness come to my relief. Do not bring your servant into judgment, for no one living is righteous before you. The enemy pursues me, he crushes me to the ground... I meditate on all your works and consider what your hands have done. I spread out my hands to you; my soul thirsts for you like a parched land.

This prayer is one of utter desperation, but there is hope precisely because it is a prayer. There is a sense that, somehow, some day, God will save. Sin is acknowledged and therefore the fact that salvation is undeserved is also acknowledged. An enemy had brought about the situation and his destruction is sought, but this is not the main emphasis. The plea is based on God's faithfulness, and his works in past times are cited as evidence of his willingness to work in a covenant relationship with repentant sinners.

The writer has learned that God does not side with the mighty but with those who understand that they are his servants. Dedication to God's service inevitably leads to confrontation with the enemies of God's people. This confrontation goes with the calling, and it is the responsibility of the one who called to provide deliverance from these enemies.

This prayer is one of many evidences in scripture that it is when our circumstances are darkest that we are most aware of our need of God and closest to his fatherly love. We come to a point where, despite continuing troubles, we know that he will act. This is where trust is exercised. The victory is here, rather than at the point when we walk out into the sunshine.

We may utter such a prayer to God when we know we are caught up in a situation we cannot control or change. I still have an epistle of despair that I wrote to God in March 2000. It began, 'Dear Lord, something has to change...' Almost exactly one year later a series of events began that led me through even darker times, but God held me and brought me to a better place.

Sunday reflection

What have you learned in your dark places? Is your church honest about its collective experiences of the dark?

AR

Living with the dilemma

O God, whom I praise, do not remain silent, for wicked and deceitful men have opened their mouths against me; they have spoken against me with lying tongues. With words of hatred they surround me; they attack me without cause. In return for my friendship they accuse me, but I am a man of prayer. They repay me evil for good, and hatred for my friendship. Appoint an evil man to oppose him; let an accuser stand at his right hand. When he is tried, let him be found guilty, and may his prayers condemn him… May no one extend kindness to him or take pity on his fatherless children.

The individual, the nation, the minority group is in the very depths. Efforts to find an honourable resolution have failed. This psalm is an admission that even though we may act in a righteous manner, we will not always be vindicated. To admit that there is no way out of a particular dilemma may seem faithless, but what these psalms are teaching us is that faith perseveres in such circumstances, at the same time refusing to sidestep life's realities.

The wicked and deceitful people referred to here were once friends, but friendship has been repaid with treachery and false accusations. A brick wall has been erected. There is no closure, so in desperation a solution is dreamed up, the rejection repaid with rejection, which is the only remaining defence mechanism. The accuser must be accused and a guilty verdict is so certain that the punishment has already been decided. The lives of the enemies and of their families to future generations must become a howling wilderness. The psalmist feels free to pronounce what is almost a series of curses (vv. 6–20). God is not addressed directly but his name is invoked. It is assumed that he will approve. The desire is expressed that God will never forgive the enemies' sins or those of their ancestors, that their curses will be turned back on them.

True maturity comes when we are able to live with the dilemma and stop dreaming up resolutions, holy or otherwise. The meaning of the word 'forgive' is to 'let go'. This psalm does not arrive at that point.

Prayer

Forgiving Lord, hold us when your ways are too high for us to emulate.

AR

Living the questions

I am poor and needy, and my heart is wounded within me… Help me, O Lord my God; save me in accordance with your love. Let them know that it is your hand, that you, O Lord, have done it. They may curse, but you will bless; when they attack they will be put to shame, but your servant will rejoice. My accusers will be clothed with disgrace and wrapped in shame as in a cloak.

How many in our world must feel like this! Many parents of youthful drug abusers must curse the suppliers. Prostitutes must long to see their unscrupulous pimps exposed. Farmers turned off their land by a new regime or a new landowner who wants to plant a more profitable cash crop, those minority groups persecuted by the majority and many betrayed by those to whom they had entrusted themselves, may dream of vindication and revenge. This psalm helps us to pray with them.

Good literature often contains pearls of great wisdom. In the novel *The Sixth Lamentation* (Time Warner, 2004) by William Brodrick, a wise monk pronounces these words: 'If you keep listening, you still don't get any answers but more often than not the questions slip out of reach and cease to be questions. The bad news is that it takes about ten years.'

The poet Rainer Maria Rilke made a plea that we learn to love the questions 'like locked rooms and like books that are written in a very foreign language… Live the questions now. Perhaps you will then gradually without noticing it, live along some distant day into the answer' (*Letters to a Young Poet*, Norton, 1993). Meanwhile, in more words from the monk in Brodrick's novel, 'all that matters are tiny reconciliations. Be reconciled whenever you get the chance.'

Where the opportunity presents itself we can move on from the desire for vindication when our minds have finally let go. Some people feel able to forgive and move on immediately. Those who find they cannot do this must not give up on themselves but continue to listen until the questions 'slip out of reach'.

Reflection

Use this psalm as a prayer as you get alongside, in your imagination, those who cannot forgive. Check your own progress in learning to live with any unanswered questions in your life.

AR

Poverty of spirit

Rescue me, O Lord, from evil men; protect me from men of violence, who devise evil plans in their hearts and stir up war every day. They make their tongues as sharp as a serpent's; the poison of vipers is on their lips. Keep me, O Lord, from the hands of the wicked; protect me from men of violence… O Lord, I say to you, 'You are my God.' Hear, O Lord, my cry for mercy. O Sovereign Lord, my strong deliverer… do not grant the wicked their desires, O Lord; do not let their plans succeed… I know that the Lord secures justice for the poor and upholds the cause of the needy. Surely the righteous will praise your name and the upright will live before you.

The harsh reality is that human beings can be very nasty. Jealousy and lust for power are rampant in our world. This is clear at a local, personal level and not just in fields of international conflict—and the Christian community is not free from this either. It is vital that we examine and recognize the state of our own hearts.

In this psalm David was a victim of violent, devious men, not the perpetrator of violence. So far as he was able, he lived an upright life and, most importantly, he recognized his poverty—that of the person who has no legitimate resources for overcoming the enemy, and refuses to use ungodly means to make up for this inadequacy. He recognizes that only God has what it takes to resolve things justly.

We may know of folk who have been or are victims of jealousy or unfaithfulness or being passed over at work. Any escape can seem better than struggling on. A good dose of vindictiveness can seem momentarily satisfying. Such temptations can be daily realities and as believers face them they may fluctuate between wishing to see the enemy hurt and the desire to trust God to bring justice and a holy outcome.

Jesus said that the kingdom belongs to the poor in spirit. It is better to mourn than to comfort ourselves by getting back at the enemy. Utter dependence on God, no matter what, is the only way to be fully human.

Prayer

God of the whole world, make me more like you.

AR

The Lord our helper

If the Lord had not been on our side—let Israel say—if the Lord had not been on our side when men attacked us, when their anger flared against us, they would have swallowed us alive; the flood would have engulfed us, the torrent would have swept over us, the raging waters would have swept us away. Praise be to the Lord, who has not let us be torn by their teeth. We have escaped like a bird out of the fowler's snare; the snare has been broken, and we have escaped. Our help is in the name of the Lord, the Maker of heaven and earth.

The plea has been made, the problem articulated and God has acted. The writer expresses the feeling of being saved in the nick of time from fire, from being eaten alive, from flood, torrent and raging waters. The anticipated trouble had not passed by. Calamity arrived on the doorstep, but in the midst of calamity God did his saving work. God heard the moans, the weeping and the sighing. He felt his people's fear and listened to their complaint. He did not turn away because they hadn't the heart for a praise party. He had taught them that he was their faithful king who would not desert them in times of trouble and in pouring out their complaints to him they had demonstrated that they believed him.

The thought of a snare does not seem so threatening as the raging waters mentioned earlier, but the innocent, tiny bird for which the trap is set is powerless unless someone intervenes and breaks the snare. There is a humble, heartfelt acknowledgement that this was the case for Israel. They had had no power to help themselves.

The statement is made that God is on our side, but here there is no claim that the help was deserved. His people are the undeserving recipients of the grace of the Maker of heaven and earth. The inference is that, if it so desires, the whole of creation may place itself under that protection. God will watch over those who do.

Prayer

Maker of heaven and earth, thank you for your ongoing care for all you have made. Thank you for caring for me, for delivering me out of trouble.

AR

Lowly is fine

I will praise you, O Lord, with all my heart; before the 'gods' I will sing your praise… When I called, you answered me; you made me bold and stout-hearted… Though the Lord is on high, he looks upon the lowly, but the proud he knows from afar. Though I walk in the midst of trouble, you preserve my life; you stretch out your hand against the anger of my foes, with your right hand you save me. The Lord will fulfil his purpose for me; your love, O Lord, endures for ever—do not abandon the works of your hands.

Things have been hard. The enemy had had the upper hand and his gods had therefore seemed more powerful, but faith in Yahweh has been vindicated. The psalmist David had prayed as king, so the prayers were for the whole of Israel rather than for himself. Nevertheless he knows that God has heard him personally and that is an important realization.

By acknowledging that it was God who had emboldened him, David admits that his own courage and strength had failed. If he had been overconfident in earlier success, he was humbled by a dilemma for which he did not possess adequate resources. It is at this point of need that God hears and answers prayer. He is elbowed out by human pride, but humble confession of need is a space in which he can move.

Much is written today about self-confidence and assertiveness. We are supposed to depend upon ourselves. Success is perceived in terms of monetary gain and the acquisition of material goods. Loss of employment is loss of status, and so on. Where Christians take up these attitudes, they are often justified in terms of God wishing to prosper his people.

God has greater desire for our holiness than for our worldly happiness and he will lead us through any number of vales of tears to secure it. In the process we shall be emptied of any reliance on self or on anything or anyone but him. If this increases in us the confidence that 'The Lord will fulfil his purposes for me', the tears will not have been shed in vain.

Reflection

Are you confident that God will fulfil his purposes for you and that they will be for your good?

AR

Remembering not to forget

Praise the Lord, O my soul; all my inmost being, praise his holy name. Praise the Lord, O my soul, and forget not all his benefits— who forgives all your sins and heals all your diseases, who redeems your life from the pit and crowns you with love and compassion, who satisfies your desires with good things so that your youth is renewed like the eagle's. The Lord works righteousness and justice for all the oppressed... The Lord is compassionate and gracious, slow to anger, abounding in love... As a father has compassion on his children, so the Lord has compassion on those who fear him.

David here shares the lessons he has learned in the pit. While the believer is sinful, subject to disease, needy and easily worn out, in answer to these weaknesses God forgives, heals, redeems and satisfies. The fulfilment of his purposes does not depend upon any goodness or strength in his people. He only requires that they obey him in faith. Where even this fails, he goes on with his redeeming activity and works for their good.

This does not mean that we may 'go on sinning so that grace may increase' (Romans 6:1). There is always a responsibility to study God's word and allow that and his Spirit to transform us. We shall need again and again to come back for forgiveness where we have been wrong and for new insights where we have misunderstood.

When we have come through difficult times we should not then put it all behind us or try to forget it. What has happened is now a part of us and always will be and if we forget, or pretend to, we shall also forget the lessons God taught us through it. We should record the ways that God redeemed us in and from the pit, or we shall lose sight of them and they will not mould our characters as they might. This is the way that situations are redeemed, rather than by pretending they never happened. The Church is richer for those who know the realities of life in this world and who have, by the grace of God, come through with a testimony to his love and compassion.

Reflection

In what ways are you in need of God's forgiveness or healing today?

AR

PSALM 113 (NIV)

Pure celebration

Praise the Lord. Praise, O servants of the Lord, praise the name of the Lord. Let the name of the Lord be praised, both now and for evermore. From the rising of the sun to the place where it sets, the name of the Lord is to be praised. The Lord is exalted over all the nations, his glory above the heavens. Who is like the Lord our God, the One who sits enthroned on high, who stoops down to look on the heavens and the earth? He raises the poor from the dust and lifts the needy from the ash heap; he seats them with princes, with the princes of their people. He settles the barren woman in her home as a happy mother of children. Praise the Lord.

This hymn of praise illustrates the impossibility of separating religion and politics. First, all nations are subject to Yahweh's rule, acknowledged or not. It is his sun that rises and sets each day and all beneath it are to praise him alone as God. He sits on the throne and all power is delegated from there. Moreover this God does not favour the powerful that use this power to their own advantage. He expects it to be used to raise the poor and needy to places of dignity suited to creatures made in his image. Beyond this, he uses his power directly where that alone will work. There are numerous biblical examples of such cases. The one cited here is that of the barren woman and those singing this hymn would immediately recall Sarah, Rebekah and Hannah, and we may add Elizabeth.

The day of celebration is for remembering how God has stooped down to help the lowly, not for boasting of the nation's strengths and superiority. There is no triumphing over the enemy, no cursing or assigning them and theirs to oblivion. All such thoughts are gone. God's love has melted hearts and attention is focused on him, who, even when angry against sin, remembers to be merciful. In our celebrations as churches, we must testify honestly to how we have acknowledged our own need and come to him for help.

Sunday reflection

How do we as church communities demonstrate God's care for those who are in physical, monetary, emotional or spiritual need?

AR

A great deliverance

When Israel came out of Egypt, the house of Jacob from a people of foreign tongue, Judah became God's sanctuary, Israel his dominion. The sea looked and fled, the Jordan turned back; the mountains skipped like rams, the hills like lambs. Why was it, O sea, that you fled, O Jordan, that you turned back, you mountains, that you skipped like rams, you hills, like lambs? Tremble, O earth, at the presence of the Lord, at the presence of the God of Jacob, who turned the rock into a pool, the hard rock into springs of water.

God's people spoke continually of the great deliverance he had brought about for them from slavery in Egypt. The awe it inspired is demonstrated supremely in this beautiful psalm. It is as though the exodus only happened yesterday. The sea, the mountains of Sinai and the Jordan river all stood in the way of God's people as they marched towards their goal, but none of these could withstand God's power. Once God's supremacy had been so mightily demonstrated, nothing could ever be the same. Every aspect of creation should now know its place.

The people of Jacob were never perfect, just like any other human grouping, like the Church today. Nevertheless, God had called them to be his people and remained faithful to his covenant with Jacob's ancestor, Abraham. Some had held the mistaken idea that because they were God's people their path would be strewn with flowers and

their enemies totally ineffective. That was never so—in Egypt, during the exodus or since—but precisely in the problems that beset them continually, they learned that he was God and were constantly reassured they were his people.

As God's people today we know we have experienced a greater deliverance—from the power of sin to decide our destiny. We have been made inheritors of God's kingdom of love. Within the covenant he has made with us, which we remember each time we share the Lord's supper, he turns the rocks of our experience into quiet pools and even springs of life-giving water. This God is to be praised by everything and everyone ever created or to be created—and he will be!

Prayer

Awesome God, may we remember always what you have done for us in Christ and praise you with our lives.

AR

The BRF
Magazine

Richard Fisher writes...

Spirituality is one of those words that means different things to different people. For some, it means meeting God in quiet contemplation; for others it's more about getting involved in the messiness of life—and finding that God is there too. Some are inspired by the insights of great disciples from ancient traditions; others learn best from the ordinary Christians they meet in the here and now.

Whatever your take on spirituality, with 2000 years of Christian heritage behind us and a living God who is still at work in the world today, we have a wealth of resources to explore. BRF is dedicated to helping you dig into those resources and journey into a deeper understanding of God and his purposes—as 'heart-knowledge', not just 'head-knowledge'.

Most of us find, though, that as we travel further into that 'heart-knowledge' of God, we come up against aspects of spirituality that are bound to remain a mystery to us until we die! Even the very centre of our faith, the death and resurrection of Jesus Christ, is one of those mysteries.

So in this issue of *The BRF Magazine*, which focuses on our core ministry of prayer and spirituality, you'll find both diversity and mystery. John Pridmore, Rector of Hackney in East London, writes about the sorrows and surprising joys of ministry in perhaps the most crime-ridden area of Britain today, while Naomi Starkey recommends books on angels and long-ago saints. An extract from this year's Lent book, *The Road to Emmaus* by Helen Julian CSF, shows how the 17th-century poet John Donne struggled with the mystery of Easter, and Martyn Payne encourages us to rescue that mystery from the 21st-century commercial fixation on fluffy animals, in our work with children.

Finally, in this issue, we extend an invitation to find out about *Foundations21—the new way to do discipleship*, which launched last year. I make no apology for including this in a magazine devoted mainly to spirituality—we are so excited about this project that I couldn't miss it out! If you haven't done so already, please order the free DVD that introduces the programme, or log on to:

www.foundations21.org.uk

Richard Fisher, Chief Executive

An extract from
The Road to Emmaus

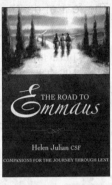

THE ROAD TO
Emmaus

Helen Julian CSF

COMPANIONS FOR THE JOURNEY THROUGH LENT

BRF's Lent book for this year offers the chance to reflect on the experiences and teaching of some key figures in English spiritual history. From a host of possible subjects, author Helen Julian CSF has chosen seven: Julian of Norwich, Thomas Traherne, the Venerable Bede, John Donne, John and Charles Wesley, Aelred of Rievaulx and the anonymous author of *The Cloud of Unknowing*. The following abridged extract is taken from the Introduction, plus readings on John Donne's understanding of death and resurrection.

Introduction

For many Christians, Lent is a time of heightened and more purposeful engagement with the many elements of the Christian life. It has, of course, a particular focus on discipline, penitence, fasting and reflection on the passion of Christ, but for many it is also a time to overhaul their prayer life, to read the scriptures in a more organized way, and to serve others more consciously.

The seven figures from British spirituality whom you will meet in this book are, I hope, good guides on this pilgrimage through Lent. Through their lives and work, Lenten themes and others can be illuminated. They are all authors, so if any become particular friends and guides to you during this Lenten journey, you can continue to travel with them after finishing this book, by exploring further their own writings.

Along the way there are opportunities to put into practice some of what the companions are offering as their particular gift… To be really effective, this book needs to be 'performed'; put into practice in ways which engage body, spirit, and mind…

The journey of this book takes you from joy, the joy of creation, through places of darkness and struggle, and places of light, encouragement and growth, to the rediscovered joy of re-creation…

Our Christian journey is never made alone, however it may sometimes feel. The great company of our fellow travellers extends through time and space; may this Lent be a time when some of these companions become real friends and guides to you.

The fear of death

Donne knew through faith that death would not have the last word, but its voice was loud in his ears. The fear of death, and an awareness of the inevitability of death, is a thread running through much of his writing… Donne was acutely aware of the brevity of life, and seems to have always felt that death was near, perhaps just round the next corner.

We are all conceived in close prison; in our mother's wombs, we are close prisoners all; when we are born, we are born but to the liberty of the house; prisoners still, though within larger walls; and then all our life is but a going out to the place of execution, to death.

… In the reflections that he wrote after his serious illness of 1623, Donne could sometimes look more calmly upon death. As he lay in bed listening to the bells tolling for others who were dying or dead, he could even see death as 'a preferment', as a translation to something better, to which he, as a member of humankind, should aspire.

But as when men see many of their own professions preferred, it ministers a hope that that may light upon them; so when these hourly bells tell me of so many funerals of men like me, it presents, if not a desire that it may, yet a comfort whensoever mine shall come.

It is the common lot of humankind to die, but as a Christian, Donne knows that in dying he will not fall out of God's hand. As in baptism he was connected to Christ, the head of the body, so in death he will not be separated from him. So the death of anyone, who is a part of the body, affects him: 'Any man's death diminishes me, because I am involved in mankind, and therefore never send to know for whom the bell tolls; it tolls for thee.' Used rightly, this kind of reflection can lead us closer to God.

Death, thou shalt die

Now if Christ is proclaimed as raised from the dead, how can some of you say there is no resurrection of the dead? If there is no resurrection of the dead, then Christ has not been raised; and if Christ has not been raised, then our proclamation has been in vain and your faith has been in vain…

But in fact Christ has been raised from the dead, the first fruits of those who have died. For since death came through a human being, the resurrection of the dead has also come through a human being; for as all die in Adam, so all will be made alive in Christ. But each in his own order: Christ the first fruits, then at his coming those who belong to Christ. Then comes the end, when he hands over the kingdom to God the Father, after he has destroyed every ruler and every authority and power. For he must reign until he has put all his enemies under his feet. The last enemy to be destroyed is death.

1 CORINTHIANS 15:12–14, 20–26

If Donne wrote vividly of the reality of death and the natural human fear of it, he wrote equally vividly of the hope of resurrection, resting on the resurrection of Christ. He imagined himself, at the resurrection of the body, saying to Christ, 'I am of the same stuff as you, body and body, flesh and flesh, and therefore let me sit down with you, at the right hand of the Father' because death, the last enemy, has been destroyed in Christ's death.

Because the new life of the resurrection is indeed new life, it is hard to describe, hard to imagine. Paul uses much of the long 15th chapter of his first letter to the Corinthians trying to explain what the resurrection will be like, and to answer some of the Corinthians' questions. He uses the image of the seed, which must die in order to come to new life. The new life is contained in the seed that is sown, but may look very different from the seed when it grows (1 Corinthians 15:36–38).

Donne too struggled to find language to describe the resurrection. As a former librarian, I particularly enjoy his image of humankind as one volume with one author. When someone dies, their chapter

'is not torn out of the book, but translated into a better language'. Various translators are employed by God—age, sickness, war, justice —'but God's hand is in every translation, and his hand shall bind up all our scattered leaves again, for that library where every book shall lie open to one another'.

In one of his sermons, Donne uses another vivid image. He sees himself as money, given in taxes to the king, and so becoming part of the royal exchequer. 'So this body… being given in subsidy, as a contribution to the glory of my God, in the grave, becomes a part of God's Exchequer.' In the same sermon, he goes on to make an important point, one that is very biblical but is often forgotten today. The angels, he says, shall rejoice 'when they shall see me in my soul, to have all that they have, and in my body, to have that that they have not'.

The Christian doctrine of the resurrection is a very earthy and physical one. We will not be disembodied spirits, but whole people, body and soul; changed indeed, no longer perishable and mortal but imperishable and immortal (1 Corinthians 15:53). Donne knew that this was a difficult thing to believe. In another sermon, he says that the immortality of the soul is easy to believe in, but the immortality of the body can only be believed by faith. He lists some of the difficulties that will be raised against this belief. How can a body, burnt a thousand years ago, ash scattered in wrinkles and furrows of the earth, be brought together again? How can a bone shattered by shot be put back together? How can a body that lost an arm in Europe and a leg in Asia be reassembled?

Only by God's power, he says. God knows 'in what part of the world every grain of every man's dust lies; and... he whispers, he hisses, he beckons for the bodies of his saints, and in the twinkling of an eye, that body that was scat-tered over all the elements, is sat down at the right hand of God, in a glorious resurrection.'

No wonder he could write, in one of his most famous sonnets:

Death, be not proud...
One short sleep past,
we wake eternally,
And death shall be no more.
Death, thou shalt die.

To order a copy of this book, please turn to page 159. See below for the full text of 'Death, be not proud'.

Holy Sonnet 10

Death, be not proud, though some have called thee
Mighty and dreadful, for thou art not so;
For those whom thou thinkst thou dost overthrow
Die not, poor Death, nor yet canst thou kill me.
From rest and sleep, which but thy pictures be,
Much pleasure—then, from thee much more must flow;
And soonest our best men with thee do go,
Rest of their bones and soul's delivery.
Thou'rt slave to fate, chance, kings, and desperate men,
And dost with poison, war, and sickness dwell;
And poppy or charms can make us sleep as well,
And better than thy stroke. Why swellst thou then?
One short sleep past, we wake eternally,
And death shall be no more. Death, thou shalt die.

Foundations21

THE NEW WAY TO DO DISCIPLESHIP

Foundations21—the new way to do discipleship offers a flexible discipleship programme that fits around your lifestyle and learning style and gives you the opportunity to grow in your faith and become a more effective disciple of Jesus Christ.

What does it offer?

- Multimedia, internet-based learning
- 4 different pathways through the programme
- Small group meetings
- Online community and discussion through message boards and chatrooms
- 1-2-1 discipleship mentoring
- Daily updates, refreshers, inspiration and challenges

Want to know more?

To find out more, log on to:

www.foundations21.org.uk

For a free promotional DVD, introduced by Adrian Plass, please complete your contact details overleaf, and return the form to BRF, First Floor, Elsfield Hall, 15–17 Elsfield Way, OXFORD, OX2 8FG

Foundations21

THE NEW WAY TO DO DISCIPLESHIP

Name

Address

Telephone

E-mail

❏ Please send me the FREE promotional DVD, introduced by Adrian Plass

❏ Please send me the Foundations21 e-zine

❏ Please send me subscription rates for subscribers to Foundations21

Please return this form to: BRF, First Floor, Elsfield Hall, 15–17 Elsfield Way, OXFORD OX2 8FG

BRF is a Registered Charity

An extract from
Quiet Spaces: The City

The current issue of *Quiet Spaces* celebrates the human creativity and diversity found in cities, and reflects on some of the challenges of city living. Both the diversity and the challenges can be seen in this abridged extract from 'Hackney: the inner city of God', by John Pridmore, Rector of Hackney in London's East End.

Hackney has been described as 'the inner city of sorrows', yet there are some who live here for whom the place, for all its woes, offers the prospect of another city.

The sorrows of Hackney are notorious. Rates of unemployment soar and many find it hard to make ends meet. Demands on social services provision are massive, and many have fallen through the welfare net. Much of the local housing, particularly on the surviving 1960s estates, is run down. Hackney bumps along the bottom of any table of social well-being you care to consult.

We have about the worst crime rate in Britain. Some time ago, a press reporter wrote about Hackney, 'There are possibly more shots fired in this area than anywhere else in Britain.' The article included a map with seven cheerful little stars on it to show where seven people had been shot dead in the previous four years. These were 'gangland executions', mostly to do with drugs, and the map was, more or less, a map of my parish...

So Hackney is challenging. But this inner city of sorrows is also the inner city of God, and I would not wish to be anywhere else. For all its problems, Hackney is a marvellously vibrant community. It... is home to many artists, writers and musicians. Creative people find it an inspiration. It boasts the East End's last and most magnificent music hall, the Hackney Empire, recently splendidly refurbished.

But what most makes Hackney resemble the city to which we are travelling on our spiritual pilgrimage is that it is home from home to everyone from everywhere. On my desk is a report on our church secondary school. The report lists the different 'first languages' spoken by our pupils: Yoruba, Twi, Cantonese, Krio, Okpe, Punjabi, Creole, Ibo, Edo, Urdu, Lingala, Russian, Hindi, and many more. I step outside my front door and walk along the street. The drycleaners are Turkish, the newsagents are Indian, the carpet store is a Jewish business, the place next door that will polish your nails is Chinese, the Afro hairdressers is run by Nigerians, the Halal butchers are Pakistani, next to them is the Vietnamese takeaway and the Greek candle shop, and so on and on. Of course there is friction, and occasionally worse than friction, but on the whole we get on with each other wonderfully well…

What about Christianity in Hackney? We still have far to go. The churches tend to wend their separate ways, many preoccupied with self-preservation. How the churches approach those outside their folds differs according to their conflicting theologies. The most significant division of opinion, however, is not over the issues that have historically separated the churches. What divides Christians in Hackney has much more to do with the neighbourhood's poverty.

The most successful church in Hackney meets in a vast converted warehouse. Recently I attended one of their services, where I found myself one of a congregation of several thousand. The preacher bounded around a platform as big as a tennis court. 'God will move against nature to bless you!' he shouts. 'No matter what the doctor says, no matter what the cancer says, you shall be blessed!'

Such churches teach that being well and being well-off are a sign of God's blessing and that illness and poverty are indicators of divine displeasure. There is another way of looking at things. This is to argue that many are poor because it suits the rich to keep them that way, and that many are ill because they cannot escape from unhealthy situations not of their making. God is not angry with the poor but on their side. Building a bridge between those who preach that Christian faith boosts your bank balance and those who, with Dietrich Bonhoeffer, warn that Christ calls us to die has so far proved beyond the skills of Hackney's ecumenical movement.

Hackney is a melée of religious communities, all telling their different stories. During my ten years here, I have come to realize how important it is to find time to listen to each other's stories. I think of a reception (kosher sherry and nibbles) held in the Mayor of Hackney's parlour in the town hall, to welcome a group of young people—Jews, Muslims and Christians—from Haifa in Israel, a city with which Hackney is twinned. I remember catching a glimpse of these teenagers sharing some private joke, perhaps about how ridiculous we oldies looked as we

> *God is not angry with the poor but on their side*

made our stuffy speeches. Clearly they were the best of friends. They were also, perhaps, a sign to us that we should aim for more than mannered courtesies in our inter-faith relationships. My worry about the different religious communities in Hackney is not only that we do not work together. It is also that we so seldom laugh together.

Thank God, Hackney people do know how to laugh. That is another reason why they are next-of-kin to the citizens of heaven. And there's plenty to laugh about, not least in our own church life. I recall my first Midnight Mass in Hackney. Six-year-old Judy was entrusted with baby Jesus and, to the singing of 'Away in a Manger', she led the procession to the crib. Her contribution to the liturgy was to drop him. 'Never mind, Judy,' I whispered. 'We'll pick him up.' 'We can't,' she said. 'His head's come off. It's gone under the piano.'…

Just as an individual must try to discover what is his or her vocation, so too must a local church seek to identify its particular calling… We have concluded that ours is a threefold vocation.

We are called, first, to be a church for the young. We heed the example of Jesus who set children at the centre of the circle of his disciples… Our calling to serve children, with whom, as with the poor,

A church for the young, the poor, all peoples

Jesus identified himself, is clear. These inner-city children are also children of the city that is to come. Of that city we read, 'the streets of the city shall be full of boys and girls playing' (Zechariah 8:5).

Second, we are called to be a church for the poor. In our church we have something quaintly called 'Hackney 180°'. This is a drop-in and advice centre, which seeks to be both a shelter and, if any wish to use it as such, a leg up to better things for the many in our neighbourhood who are homeless… We see our social care work not as a project that is somehow 'bolted on' to the main fabric of our life but as integral to it.

Third, we are called to be a church for all peoples… Our longing is that our church should not be a ghetto but a fellowship open and attentive to the insights of all who seek for truth and who bear witness to that truth from the vantage points of their own traditions. As well as sharing our 'good news', we must seek the common ground on which we can work together to serve our neighbourhood.

We're still far from heaven, but there's enough about Hackney for the rumours of that other city to ring true.

To order a copy of Quiet Spaces: The City *or previous issues, please turn to the order form on page 159.*

The Editor recommends...

Naomi Starkey

Introduce the word 'spirituality' into a conversation these days, and chances are that the word 'angels' will crop up at some point. While the idea of angels has always intrigued a good number of people, interest in the subject has grown enormously in recent years. From stories of mysterious encounters with helpful strangers (who then disappear into thin air) to fascination with the idea of guardian angels, many are attracted to the notion of divine intervention and protection, even if they have little or no interest in the Christian faith.

In *Assist our Song*, author Carol Hathorne takes a look at what the Bible has to say about angels and also shares a host of stories of 'angelic experiences', many of which she has personally gathered in the course of her ministry in local churches. She considers such questions as 'Who are angels and what do they do?', 'In what ways can they help us as Christians?' and 'Are they always shining beings with wings, or can ordinary people in some way be angels too?'

While she shows that both Old and New Testaments present angels as messengers, guardians and even travelling companions, she stresses how we must always keep in mind the biblical insistence on angels as servants of God. In contrast to the suggestions of many New Age angel books, websites and so on, the Bible stresses that we should never try to access these beings as separate sources of spiritual power or protection.

Assist our Song is an ideal book for anybody wanting an introduction to the subject of angels, whether a committed Christian, newly come to faith or simply somebody on the fringes of the Church and intrigued by the subject. It has been warmly endorsed by Jennifer Rees Larcombe, who describes it as 'not only an inspiring Bible study but also a grippingly good read'.

Carol Hathorne's name will be familiar to many, as she has written some 18 books, including *The Accidental Church* (Kingsway, 2003), *Christian Dance* (Monarch, 1999), *Angels Keep Watch* (Christina Press, 1997) and *A Ferret in the Vestry* (Monarch, 1995). She is Assistant Minister at a West Midlands Anglican church, and is also married to a vicar.

In popular thinking, the topic of angels has tended to absorb a lot of the interest previously shown in saints. In *Living the Gospel*, Helen Julian CSF explores the life and teaching of the man whom many people would probably name when asked for a 'favourite saint': St Francis. He is an enduringly popular figure, who continues to have a wide appeal today because of the way his teaching challenges the values of modern consumer-driven culture—and because of his love of animals!

Not only does the book explore St Francis, however, but it also introduces the spirituality of St Clare to a wider audience. Comparatively little-known, she was a surprisingly influential female spiritual leader who joined with Francis as early as 1212 (he began his work in 1208). After his death, she became the holder of his vision for the whole Franciscan movement, particularly keen to maintain the emphasis on poverty that had been central to his teaching.

Author Helen Julian CSF is an Anglican Franciscan sister, a member of the Community of St Francis and presently serving the community as Minister Provincial. She is a popular contributor to BRF's *New Daylight* notes and has also written *The Lindisfarne Icon* about St Cuthbert (now out of print). In the concluding chapter of *Living the Gospel*, she shares a little of her story of how she came to take life vows in the Community. It all began with a weekend visit to a Franciscan friary, which happened to offer hospitality in the village she was visiting!

She summarizes the initial appeal of the Franciscans: 'It was something about the way the brothers were with each other and with their guests—human, real, deeply serious about the things of God but with joy and humour, and thoroughly engaged with the everyday realities of life.'

Her latest book is BRF's Lent book for 2007, *The Road to Emmaus*, which was published last November. Subtitled 'Companions for the journey through Lent', this book offers a chance to reflect, day by day, on the experiences and teaching of some key figures in English spiritual history (see the extract on pages 139–142).

The book shares something of the life stories of each character, and provides information on their historical context, besides considering the themes unique to their writings. This is all linked to relevant Bible passages, and suggestions for imaginative ways to put into practice what we have learnt.

To order copies of the BRF books recommended here, please turn to the order form on page 159.

Making the most of Easter with children

Martyn Payne

I wonder whether you have ever stopped to reflect on the commercial litany of the card shop between New Year and Easter? In January, the displays put away their Christmas and New Year stock only to replace them with the hearts and flowers of approaching Valentine's Day. Once the Feast of Young Love is past, it is the celebration of motherhood that hits the shop windows, with ever-bigger cards to say 'thank you' at the Feast of All Souls Maternal.

Finally, we come to the Feast of All Things Fluffy. Rabbits and chickens hop and cheep among the serried ranks of cards for sale urging us to make the most of the Feast of the New Born... Animals. And yes, of course, there are eggs by the dozen, though in fact that tempting creme egg has already been crying out for our attention from early January to prepare us for Resurr-egg-tion Day!

Where once the year was marked by the feasts and festivals of the Church, to remind us that there is more to life than just the passing of days and months, now we have commercial time to shape the calendar of our lives. Is this all that our children will remember? And don't we have much more to offer them than this?

Even in our churches, there is an increasing tendency to lose touch with the alternative way of marking time that the cycle of our faith stories can give us. This is particularly so, of course, when some of those festival moments fall during the week, such as Candlemas or Ash Wednesday, or where churches have gone in for sermon series that are more concerned to teach particular doctrines than to follow the story. This can mean that all of us, and particularly children, are swept on in a disconnected way from Jesus in the manger to Jesus on the cross in just a few months.

The great events of Holy Week and Easter didn't just happen out of the blue as this can so easily suggest, but they developed slowly, particularly during those important weeks of Lent, and we owe it to our children to help them to get ready for this amazing moment that changed the world for ever.

Whatever resources you use with

your children, can I urge you to make sure that Easter does not just come suddenly and unexpectedly for your group. Ideally, at least the Sundays in Lent—the six weeks leading up to Easter—should be a time to focus on the life and teaching of Jesus. Why not spend time exploring some of the miracles and parables to help children get ready for that momentous week when Jesus knew he had to go to Jerusalem for the last time; the moment when he surprised everyone with a final parable and miracle that broke the power of death and robbed sin of its victory for ever.

Superheroes don't, by and large, let themselves be killed

However, this kind of language about Easter highlights another important consideration when it comes to making the most of this festival with children. How can we present such a mystery to children (or, I hear you whisper under your breath, to adults too)? Surely a defeat is a defeat. The superheroes of the children's world don't, by and large, let themselves be killed. They don't go all weak and feeble on us. They don't get humiliated and crushed like Jesus did.

There is one response to this problem, which is understandable but dangerous—namely, to skip over the difficult bit, the ugly part, and direct all our attention on to the events of Easter morning. Now of course, we must make the most

of that glorious day. The resurrection is the vital heartbeat of the gospel message, but at the same time we must not forget that its glory comes *because* of what went before, not despite it. The defeated Christ of Good Friday and the victorious Christ of Easter morning are two sides of the same coin, the two halves of the Easter message which cannot be divided. We need both the empty cross and the crucifix to comprehend fully the love of God for us. So let's not leave out half the story with our children!

I would urge every children's leader to press their minister hard to involve the children in every possible way in marking the events of Holy Week and Good Friday as much as Easter Day. Good Friday has been in the past, and is still in some churches, felt to be too dreadful, too serious and too adult a day to involve children. And so they have been left out. But the result of that approach is a resurrection without a death! No, we must tell the children the whole story. In fact, they will surprise you by being able to enter it far more fully than you thought they could.

Children already know about the dark side—about betrayal, anger, hurt, fear and death. And if we do not tell them that God loves us so much that he is ready to dive into the midst of all this darkness so that he might both share it and transform it for us, we're being neither honest about where children are (and, of course, will increasingly be as they grow up) nor honest and faithful in proclaiming what God has done.

But surely we can't tackle all the awfulness of what crucifixion means when children are present? Of course, there is so much about that dreadful form of execution that could be said, but in fact I would question whether we need to dwell on every detail, even with adults. Interestingly, the Gospel writers (in contrast to the recent filmmaker) did not dwell on the terrible pain of that day. It was what it meant that mattered, and that it really did happen—and, as in the best horror movies, the worst parts are left to our imagination. So much can be said in just a few words and with appropriate space and silence. This is the moment when history turned a corner, the moment when the unimaginable happened, and so, as the words of an ancient anthem urge us, it is rather a time for all flesh to keep silent.

It has always been strange that in comparison with the 'full-frontal' activities surrounding the celebration of Christmas, Easter has suffered by contrast and been seen as a rather child-unfriendly festival. This is how the world has chosen to dumb down this mysterious event that is central to our faith, happy simply to 'bunny' away the real meaning of this Feast of Feasts. But we must not give in to a watering down of Easter or opt out of telling our children the whole story. They need to hear about the climax of God's rescue plan for their lives; they need to hear that sacrifice is the strongest superhero weapon of all, and to hear that life comes only out of death. This is a mystery for all of us but it is at the heart of what we believe. In fact, children are far less likely to misunderstand or reject it than we think. After all, Jesus tells us that the deepest mysteries of the kingdom are more likely to be understood by children than by adults, so we should not be afraid to talk with them about it, acknowledging that we too don't know all the answers.

We have to have the whole story to begin to appreciate the love of God—a love that is revealed both in the darkness of Good Friday and the dazzling glory of Easter Day. So let us prayerfully look for ways this Easter of passing on this story to our children as of first importance, and certainly well before we start thinking about which card and Easter egg to buy!

Martyn Payne is a member of BRF's Barnabas Ministry team and co-author with Betty Pedley of A-cross the World, *published by BRF in 2004.*

A fuller version of this article, along with other ideas to help you in your work with children, can be found at:
www.barnabasinchurches.org.uk

Why not give a gift subscription this Easter?

When you take out a gift subscription to *New Daylight*, the recipient receives a FREE copy of *Long Wandering Prayer* by David Hansen with their first edition.

'This book is a breath of fresh air to those of us who become distracted when we pray and end up feeling guilt-ridden because we have not prayed enough… this is Brother Lawrence's Practising the Presence of God *for the 21st century.'*

FROM THE FOREWORD BY ANNE HIBBERT

To order your subscription, please turn to page 158.

New Daylight © BRF 2007

The Bible Reading Fellowship
First Floor, Elsfield Hall, 15–17 Elsfield Way, Oxford OX2 8FG
Tel: 01865 319700; Fax: 01865 319701
E-mail: enquiries@brf.org.uk; Website: www.brf.org.uk

ISBN-10: 1 84101 373 0
ISBN-13: 978 1 84101 373 2

Distributed in Australia by:
Willow Connection, PO Box 288, Brookvale, NSW 2100.
Tel: 02 9948 3957; Fax: 02 9948 8153;
E-mail: info@willowconnection.com.au
Available also from all good Christian bookshops in Australia.
For individual and group subscriptions in Australia:
Mrs Rosemary Morrall, PO Box W35, Wanniassa, ACT 2903.

Distributed in New Zealand by:
Scripture Union Wholesale, PO Box 760, Wellington
Tel: 04 385 0421; Fax: 04 384 3990; E-mail: suwholesale@clear.net.nz

Distributed in Canada by:
The Anglican Book Centre, 80 Hayden Street, Toronto, Ontario, M4Y 3G2
Tel: 001 416 924-1332; Fax: 001 416 924-2760;
E-mail: abc@anglicanbookcentre.com; Website: www.anglicanbookcentre.com

Publications distributed to more than 60 countries

Acknowledgments
The New Revised Standard Version of the Bible, Anglicized Edition, copyright © 1989, 1995 by the
Division of Christian Education of the National Council of the Churches of Christ in the USA. Used
by permission. All rights reserved.

The Holy Bible, New International Version, copyright © 1973, 1978, 1984, 1995 by International Bible
Society. Used by permission of Hodder & Stoughton Publishers, a division of Hodder Headline Ltd.
All rights reserved. 'NIV' is a registered trademark of International Bible Society. UK trademark
number 1448790.

The Holy Bible, Today's New International Version, copyright © 2004 by International Bible Society.
Used by permission of Hodder & Stoughton Publishers, a division of Hodder Headline Ltd. All
rights reserved. 'TNIV' is a registered trademark of International Bible Society.

New International Reader's Version, copyright © 1996, 1998 by International Bible Society. All rights
reserved throughout the world. Used by permission of International Bible Society.

The Revised Common Lectionary is copyright © The Consultation on Common Texts, 1992 and is
reproduced with permission. *The Christian Year: Calendar, Lectionary and Collects*, which includes the
Common Worship lectionary (the Church of England's adaptations of the *Revised Common Lectionary*,
published as the Principal Service lectionary) is copyright © The Central Board of Finance of the
Church of England, 1995, 1997, and material from it is reproduced with permission.

Printed in Singapore by Craft Print International Ltd

BRF is a Christian charity committed to resourcing the spiritual journey of adults and children alike. For adults, BRF publishes Bible reading notes and books and offers an annual programme of quiet days and retreats. Under its children's imprint *Barnabas*, BRF publishes a wide range of books for those working with children under 11 in school, church and home. BRF's *Barnabas Ministry* team offers INSET sessions for primary teachers, training for children's leaders in church, quiet days, and a range of events to enable children themselves to engage with the Bible and its message.

We need your help if we are to make a real impact on the local church and community. In an increasingly secular world people need even more help with their Bible reading, their prayer and their discipleship. We can do something about this, but our resources are limited. With your help, if we all do a little, together we can make a huge difference.

How can you help?

- You could support BRF's ministry with a donation or standing order (using the response form overleaf).

- You could consider making a bequest to BRF in your will, and so give lasting support to our work. (We have a leaflet available with more information about this, which can be requested using the form overleaf.)

- And, most important of all, you could support BRF with your prayers.

Whatever you can do or give, we thank you for your support.

BRF – resourcing your spiritual journey

BRF MINISTRY APPEAL RESPONSE FORM

Name _____

Address _____

_____ Postcode _____

Telephone _____ Email _____

(tick as appropriate)

Gift Aid Declaration

❑ I am a UK taxpayer. I want BRF to treat as Gift Aid Donations all donations I make from 6 April 2000 until I notify you otherwise.

Signature _____ Date _____

❑ I would like to support BRF's ministry with a regular donation by standing order (please complete the Banker's Order below).

Standing Order – Banker's Order

To the Manager, Name of Bank/Building Society _____

Address _____

_____ Postcode _____

Sort Code _____ Account Name _____

Account No _____

Please pay Royal Bank of Scotland plc, London Drummonds Branch, 49 Charing Cross, London SW1A 2DX (Sort Code 16-00-38), for the account of BRF A/C No. 00774151

The sum of _____ pounds on ___ /___ /___ (insert date your standing order starts) and thereafter the same amount on the same day of each month until further notice.

Signature _____ Date _____

Single donation

❑ I enclose my cheque/credit card/Switch card details for a donation of

£5 £10 £25 £50 £100 £250 (other) £ _____ to support BRF's ministry

Credit/ Switch card no. ❑❑❑❑❑❑❑❑❑❑❑❑❑❑❑❑❑❑❑❑

Expires ❑❑ ❑❑   Issue no. of Switch card ❑❑❑

Signature _____ Date _____

(Where appropriate, on receipt of your donation, we will send you a Gift Aid form)

❑ Please send me information about making a bequest to BRF in my will.

Please detach and send this completed form to: Richard Fisher, BRF, First Floor, Elsfield Hall, 15–17 Elsfield Way, Oxford OX2 8FG. BRF is a Registered Charity (No.233280)

ND0107

NEW DAYLIGHT SUBSCRIPTIONS

Please note our subscription rates 2007–2008. From the May 2007 issue, the new subscription rates will be:

Individual subscriptions covering 3 issues for under 5 copies, payable in advance (including postage and packing):

	UK	SURFACE	AIRMAIL
NEW DAYLIGHT each set of 3 p.a.	£12.75	£14.10	£16.35
NEW DAYLIGHT 3-year sub i.e. 9 issues	£30.00	N/A	N/A
(Not available for Deluxe edition)			
NEW DAYLIGHT DELUXE each set of 3 p.a.	£17.10	£20.70	£25.20

Group subscriptions covering 3 issues for 5 copies or more, sent to ONE address (post free):

NEW DAYLIGHT	£10.50	each set of 3 p.a.
NEW DAYLIGHT DELUXE	£14.97	each set of 3 p.a.

Please note that the annual billing period for Group Subscriptions runs from 1 May to 30 April.

Copies of the notes may also be obtained from Christian bookshops:

NEW DAYLIGHT	£3.50 each copy
NEW DAYLIGHT DELUXE	£4.99 each copy

❑ I would like to take out a subscription myself (complete your name and
   address details only once)

❑ I would like to give a gift subscription (please complete both name and
   address sections below), with a FREE copy of *Long Wandering Prayer*.

Your name _____

Your address _____

_____ Postcode _____

Gift subscription name _____

Gift subscription address _____

_____ Postcode _____

Please send *New Daylight* beginning with the May / September 2007 /
January 2008 issue: (delete as applicable)

(please tick box)	UK	SURFACE	AIR MAIL
NEW DAYLIGHT	❑ £12.75	❑ £14.10	❑ £16.35
NEW DAYLIGHT 3-year sub	❑ £30.00		
NEW DAYLIGHT DELUXE	❑ £17.10	❑ £20.70	❑ £25.20

I would like to take out an annual subscription to *Quiet Spaces* beginning
with the next available issue:

(please tick box)	UK	SURFACE	AIR MAIL
QUIET SPACES	❑ £16.95	❑ £18.45	❑ £20.85

Please complete the payment details below and send your coupon, with
appropriate payment, to: **BRF, First Floor, Elsfield Hall, 15–17 Elsfield Way,
Oxford OX2 8FG**.

Total enclosed £ _____ (cheques should be made payable to 'BRF')

Payment by cheque ❑ postal order ❑ Visa ❑ Mastercard ❑ Switch ❑

Card number: ❑❑❑❑❑❑❑❑❑❑❑❑❑❑❑❑

Expiry date of card: ❑❑❑❑   Issue number (Switch): ❑❑❑❑

Signature (essential if paying by credit/Switch card) _____

❑ Please do not send me further information about BRF publications.

BRF resources are available from your local Christian bookshop. BRF is a Registered Charity

BRF PUBLICATIONS ORDER FORM

Please ensure that you complete and send off both sides of this order form.

Please send me the following book(s):

		Quantity	Price	Total
442 7	The Road to Emmaus (Helen Julian CSF)	_____	£7.99	_____
126 6	Living the Gospel (Helen Julian CSF)	_____	£5.99	_____
446 X	Assist Our Song (C. Hathorne)	_____	£6.99	_____
264 5	A-cross the World (M. Payne & B. Pedley)	_____	£15.99	_____
503 2	Messy Church (L. Moore)	_____	£7.99	_____
399 4	Living Church (M. McBride)	_____	£9.99	_____
415 X	Quiet Spaces: Creation and Creativity (ed. B. Winter)	_____	£3.99*	_____
448 6	Quiet Spaces: The Journey (ed. B. Winter)	_____	£4.99	_____
449 4	Quiet Spaces: The Feast (ed. B. Winter)	_____	£4.99	_____
450 8	Quiet Spaces: The Garden (ed. N. Starkey)	_____	£4.99	_____
482 6	Quiet Spaces: The Wilderness (ed. N. Starkey)	_____	£4.99	_____
483 4	Quiet Spaces: The City (ed. N. Starkey)	_____	£4.99	_____
047 2	PBC: Ephesians to Colossians & Philemon (M. Maxwell)	_____	£7.99	_____
073 1	PBC: 2 Corinthians (A. Besançon Spencer)	_____	£7.99	_____
065 0	PBC: Psalms 73—150 (D. Coggan)	_____	£7.99	_____
095 2	PBC: Joshua & Judges (S. Mathewson)	_____	£7.99	_____

Total cost of books £ _____

Postage and packing (see over) £ _____

TOTAL £ _____

* Introductory offer

See over for payment details. All prices are correct at time of going to press, are subject to the prevailing rate of VAT and may be subject to change without prior warning.

BRF resources are available from your local Christian bookshop. BRF is a Registered Charity

PAYMENT DETAILS

Please complete the payment details below and send with appropriate payment and completed order form to:

**BRF, First Floor, Elsfield Hall,
15–17 Elsfield Way, Oxford OX2 8FG**

Name _____

Address _____

_____

_____ Postcode _____

Telephone _____

Email _____

Total enclosed £ _____(cheques should be made payable to 'BRF')

Payment by cheque ❏ postal order ❏ Visa ❏ Mastercard ❏ Switch ❏

Card number: ⬚⬚⬚⬚⬚⬚⬚⬚⬚⬚⬚⬚⬚⬚⬚⬚⬚⬚⬚⬚

Expiry date of card: ⬚⬚⬚⬚   Issue number (Switch): ⬚⬚⬚⬚

Signature (essential if paying by credit/Switch card) _____

ALTERNATIVE WAYS TO ORDER

Christian bookshops: All good Christian bookshops stock BRF publications. For your nearest stockist, please contact BRF.

order value	UK	Europe	Surface	Air Mail
£7.00 & under	£1.25	£3.00	£3.50	£5.50
£7.01–£30.00	£2.25	£5.50	£6.50	£10.00
Over £30.00	free	prices on request		

POSTAGE AND PACKING CHARGES

Telephone: The BRF office is open between 09.15 and 17.30. To place your order, phone 01865 319700; fax 01865 319701.

Web: Visit www.brf.org.uk

❏ Please do not send me further information about BRF publications.

BRF is a Registered Charity

ND0107